Out on Waters

HORIZONS *IN* RELIGIOUS EDUCATION is a book series sponsored by the Religious Education Association: An Association of Professors, Practitioners and Researchers in Religious Education. It was established to promote new scholarship and exploration in the academic field of Religious Education. The series will include both seasoned educators and newer scholars and practitioners just establishing their academic writing careers.

Books in this series reflect religious and cultural diversity, educational practice, living faith, and the common good of all people. They are chosen on the basis of their contributions to the vitality of religious education around the globe. Writers in this series hold deep commitments to their own faith traditions, yet their work sets forth claims that might also serve other religious communities, strengthen academic insight, and connect the pedagogies of religious education to the best scholarship of numerous cognate fields.

The posture of the Religious Education Association has always been ecumenical and multi-religious, attuned to global contexts, and committed to affecting public life. These values are grounded in the very institutions, congregations, and communities that transmit religious faith. The association draws upon the interdisciplinary richness of religious education connecting theological, spiritual, religious, social science and cultural research and wisdom. Horizons of Religious Education aims to heighten understanding and appreciation of the depth of scholarship resident within the discipline of religious education, as well as the ways it impacts our common life in a fragile world. Without a doubt, we are inspired by the wonder of teaching and the awe that must be taught.

Jack L. Seymour (co-chair), Garrett-Evangelical Theological Seminary

Dean G. Blevins (co-chair), Nazarene Theological Seminary

Elizabeth Caldwell (co-chair), McCormick Theological Seminary

Dori Grinenko Baker, The Fund for Theological Education & Sweet Briar College

Sondra H. Matthaei, Saint Paul School of Theology

Siebren Miedema, Vrije Universiteit Amsterdam

Hosffman Ospino, Boston College

Mai-Anh Le Tran, Eden Theological Seminary

Anne Streaty Wimberly, Interdenominational Theological Seminary

Out on Waters

The Religious Life and Learning of Young Catholics Beyond the Church

JAMES MICHAEL NAGLE

◆PICKWICK *Publications* • Eugene, Oregon

OUT ON WATERS
The Religious Life and Learning of Young Catholics Beyond the Church

Horizons in Religious Education Series

Copyright © 2020 James Michael Nagle. All rights reserved. Except for brief quotations in critical publications or reviews, no part of this book may be reproduced in any manner without prior written permission from the publisher. Write: Permissions, Wipf and Stock Publishers, 199 W. 8th Ave., Suite 3, Eugene, OR 97401.

Pickwick Publications
An Imprint of Wipf and Stock Publishers
199 W. 8th Ave., Suite 3
Eugene, OR 97401

www.wipfandstock.com

PAPERBACK ISBN: 978-1-7252-5579-1
HARDCOVER ISBN: 978-1-7252-5580-7
EBOOK ISBN: 978-1-7252-5581-4

Cataloguing-in-Publication data:

Names: Nagle, James Michael, author.

Title: Out on waters : the religious life and learning of young Catholics beyond the church / by James Michael Nagle.

Description: Eugene, OR: Pickwick Publications, 2020 | Series: Horizons in Religious Education | Includes bibliographical references.

Identifiers: ISBN 978-1-7252-5579-1 (paperback) | ISBN 978-1-7252-5580-7 (hardcover) | ISBN 978-1-7252-5581-4 (ebook)

Subjects: LCSH: Catholic Church—Education—United States | Catholic schools—United States | Christian education | Ex-church members—Catholic Church

Classification: LC501 N34 2020 (print) | LC501 (ebook)

Manufactured in the U.S.A.   03/23/20

CONTENTS

Series Foreword | vii
Editorial Review Board | ix
Author's Preface | xi
Introduction: Listening Without Exception: Are There Alternatives to Affiliation with the Church? | xv

Chapter 1: Like Water or Like Rock? Religious Affiliation in Today's Context of Education and Ministry | 1

Portraits from the Edge of Affiliation

Chapter 2: The Thinker and the Guide | 29
Chapter 3: The Doer and the Mystic | 56
Chapter 4: The Disaffiliating Teacher | 84

The Edge That Is a Place

Chapter 5: Deconversion and a Durable Good | 101
Chapter 6: Why Deconversion Matters: A Practical Discussion for Ministries with Young Adults | 116

Bibliography | 125

SERIES FOREWORD

We are pleased to announce this fifth book in the REA *HORIZONS* series. Dr. James Michael Nagle, who teaches at Xavier High School in New York City, addresses the growing group of people in North America called "nones," or "dones," or more officially "disaffiliated." While the research for the book is rooted in Catholic education, the reality he explores mirrors the experiences of many across the globe. We therefore believe his lively portraits, empathetic listening, and suggestions for conversation and engagement will be broadly useful to educators.

Using the qualitative research method of portraiture, James Nagle introduces us to several persons, trained in Catholic schools and knowledgeable about faith, who have disaffiliated from the church. As you read, you will come to respect these integrous people who draw on their religious training, probe their religious heritages, and are committed to serving others and making a difference in the world. While others have researched similar groups, some have focused on reclaiming them for the church and others have simply described them. Dr. Nagle goes further, asking his informants: How do religious educators work with those who have become disaffiliated?

As you will learn, open (even affirming) curiosity draws researcher and informant together into conversations touched by religious heritages and the hope of personal and social transformation. In fact, he has learned from his informants that Catholic schools are a vital place where both the religiously affiliated and disaffiliating regularly meet. The disaffiliated, Dr. Nagle has discovered, have much to teach us about religious values, about institutional failures, and about opportunities to continue to impact the wider world with religious meanings and values.

SERIES FOREWORD

The Religious Education Association has always been committed to engaging public life and to learning how values developed out of vital religious communities affect public discourse. We thank James Nagle for reminding us of this agenda and of inviting us to make a difference. Of course, some in the field of religious education focus on how persons are "formed" in a religious faith, and others explore how religious institutions from synagogues and churches to religious schools introduce people to religious belief, practice, ethical living, and community. Still others seek to understand how religious perspectives emerge in public life and how they engage public meanings. As James Nagle proposes, the encounters portrayed in this research suggest a "praxis" approach to teaching religion that draws religious life and learning as it listens to the realities of everyday life.

We commend this book to you. We invite you to listen to those who are "none," "done," or "disaffiliating," as well as those who affiliate and draw their meanings from the well of religious communities. James Nagle illustrates the power of portraiture as a mode of research. Furthermore, we learn how portraiture itself can become a mode of religious learning in which people together share how meanings, values, and actions make a difference. He asks others to extend his contextual research across traditions and cultures. He offers more affirmative ways to speak of and with those who are learning to leave the church—so that conversations can continue and we can learn together.

—Jack L. Seymour, Professor Emeritus, Garrett-Evangelical Theological Seminary, Evanston, Illinois, USA. Co-chair, Horizons Editorial Board.

—Hosffman Ospino, Boston College, Boston, Massachusetts, USA. Co-chair, Horizons Editorial Board.

—Mai-Anh Le Tran, Garrett-Evangelical Theological Seminary, Evanston, Illinois, USA. Co-chair, Horizons Editorial Board.

HORIZONS in RELIGIOUS EDUCATION— EDITORIAL REVIEW BOARD

Class of 2020

—Dean G. Blevins, Nazarene Theological Seminary, Kansas City, MO, USA.

—N. Lynne Westfield, Wabash Center for Teaching and Learning in Theology and Religion, Crawfordsville, IN, USA.

—Maureen O'Brien, Duquesne University, Pittsburgh, PA, USA.

Class of 2021

—Elizabeth Conde-Frazier, Association for Hispanic Theological Education, Orlando, FL, USA.

—Sheryl Kujawa-Holbrook, Claremont School of Theology, Claremont, CA, USA.

—Boyung Lee, Iliff School of Theology, Denver, CO, USA.

Class of 2022

—Deborah Court, Bar Ilan University, Ramat Gan, Israel

—Harold Horell, Fordham University, The Bronx, NY, USA.

—Katherine Turpin, Iliff School of Theology, Denver, CO, USA.

AUTHOR'S PREFACE

When I began formation as a Franciscan, the educators responsible for my classmates and me stated explicitly, "Even if you decide to leave this community, we believe you will benefit from the process—and so will the world." The decline in religious affiliation in the United States, particularly among young Catholics, presents a similar question to more general religious educators and theologians: Is it possible for people to benefit from leaving their religious communities? Moreover, is it possible for the tradition itself to benefit and grow in and through that process?

I did leave vowed religious life. And, as my formators had suggested, my religious education was successful. Similarly, I now wonder whether the rise of religious disaffiliation may represent something more than a failure of religious education and evangelization, seductive secular culture, or young adult narcissism.

The questions I explore are drawn from this personal journey as well as my professional experiences. I have taught religious studies and theology, directed retreats, and led service-learning programs in high schools and universities for over ten years. I love teaching religion in all these forms. I have found it to be my vocation. I explain it by recalling Gautama Buddha telling his disciples they must learn to apply his teachings in an intelligent manner and in varied situations. His teachings, he explains, are like a finger pointing at the moon, or like "a raft that carries you to the other shore." The raft is needed, but the raft is something intermediate rather than the ultimate.

Part of the vocation of teaching religion does include witnessing students deconstruct, reconstruct, and at times leave behind the raft we have built together. The portraits presented here affirm this assessment,

Author's Preface

and suggest that in our era of "liquid modernity," an expanded language is needed to include potential positive transgressions of once essential boundaries in and through religious education.

As teachers in Catholic high schools, my colleagues and I observe that some of our strongest students have taken the faithful but critical reflection we are teaching in alternative directions, including by disaffiliating from the religious communities in which they were raised. In presenting a series of research portraits, this book explores this shared observation.

How did I create those portraits? Having piloted the research design with former colleagues and students, I then met with religious educators in New York City to develop a list of effective teachers interested in discussing the phenomenon of disaffiliation. In turn, I asked them if they could identify a former student whom they had had a positive experience teaching but who nonetheless had disaffiliated from the Catholic Church. Most could.

I next reached out to the former students and invited them to participate in the study and to join their former teachers in a final group interview. I met individually with each participant, both teacher and student, for a series of open-ended, in-depth interviews and participant observations, and I conducted informal interviews with colleagues and family members of these participants before bringing the pairs together for a final group conversation.

The book focuses on six of these research participants: two teacher-learner pairs, and a pair of educators. Their challenging and inspiring conversations make the complexity of disaffiliation more comprehensible. This unique way of entering into the experience of religious life and learning today offers insight into how both educators and disaffiliating students critically and faithfully construct meaning together.

You may have trouble with some of the ideas that surface in the qualitative research and that I develop in later analysis. If you do, I nonetheless hope that through the dialogue portrayed in this book, those whom critics once described as "lost" may themselves suggest better ways to discuss their experiences, identities, and practices. This listening and this willingness to try on new and more affirming theological language to communicate what we discover together is an important first step in acknowledging that the significant movement of religious disaffiliation today involves more a leaving than a definitive loss.

Author's Preface

To begin this challenging conversation, I offer a few of the questions I gave the educator research participants prior to and during their encounter with their former students.

- If you are a professional or volunteer religious educator, how or when do most feel you have done your job successfully?
- What aspects of your tradition and religious identity do you most care about handing on?
- How do you encourage in your students a religiousness that arises from the interplay of multiple ideas, perspectives, and human experiences?
- Do you hope to equip students to contend with and afford diversity and permanent religious difference—maybe even more than one right account? If so, how do you teach such theological reflection?
- Is affiliation your goal? If not, what might be an educational or theological alternative?

These questions reflect the professional and personal journey I refer to above. Like many of the young adults I have taught, I have experienced both sides of affiliation and now reside somewhere in between. I locate myself on the outskirts of Catholicism but have mutually critical and enhancing relationships with both religiously affiliated, disaffiliating, and non-Christian individuals and communities. I feel accountable to these diverse groups and hope to contribute to a discourse that is more than a narrative of loss when speaking of and with those outside the boundaries of normative Christian practice. I critique the hegemonic "theology of affiliation" view that produces the aforementioned narrative of loss. I do so because I identify with and feel empathy toward those whose lives bear the mark of deficiency when others describe them as "Lapsed," "Fallen Away," or "Former" Catholics.

Like other kinds of portraiture, the portraits that follow make space for you to come face to face, through written language, with my research participants. But because I needed to build trust with each participant in order for each one to share with me his or her life and allow me to observe their teaching work, you will, I am sure, understand why I have disguised their identities.

INTRODUCTION

Listening Without Exception: Are There Alternatives to Affiliation with the Church?

In 2018, the Saint Mary's Press study *Going, Going, Gone* set out to improve the Catholic Church's understanding of the dynamic realities of young people who decide to disaffiliate from the Roman Catholic Church. In collaboration with the Center for Applied Research in the Apostolate (CARA), its researchers asked what appears to be a simple question: "Do we know who disaffiliates are?" The apparent admission that we don't suggests the complexity and contested nature of the conversation itself. *Going, Going, Gone* then asked an even more provocative and humble question: "Do we miss them when they are gone?" The question implies that we don't but we should.

This mainstream Catholic study concedes that a blind spot has limited the discourse among researchers and pastoral professionals. Why? Because our assumption has been that disaffiliates, and their experience, represent a problem for the church to solve. Such researchers and church professionals see returning to the church as the only faithful option because disaffiliates have "fallen way."[1]

Going, Going, Gone only touches the surface of this controversial subject, but nonetheless represents a first step in a significant alternative approach. The more positive curiosity implied in the guiding questions invite closer, more affirming empirical research that may reveal other options and reframe the conversation. This effort presents an exciting but also challenging opportunity. The Catholic community is already making some efforts to respond to that opportunity.

1. Wuerl, *New Evangelization*.

Introduction

The 2018 Synod on Young People, the Faith, and Discernment gathered to listen to young adults "without exception."[2] This timely and inspired initiative seemed to be a sign of more open dialogue with many marginal groups in the church. The Synod's final document calls young people one of the "theological places" in which G*d[3] reveals him/herself. However, the barriers implied in *Going, Going, Gone* to fulfill the goal of listening without exception clearly remain. The documents produced by the Synod, for example, continue to speak of young (and not so young) disaffiliating adults in language of loss and deficiency. Moreover, disaffiliating young Catholics themselves—the group one bishop at the Synod called "priority one"—were not in fact prioritized (in that they were not represented) at the Synod's listening sessions. As a result, the discourse remains preoccupied with this group as the target of strategies to recapture the "Lost," "Lapsed" or those who have "Fallen away."[4] This effort still speaks *of* and not *with* such persons.

Not being invited to the conversation and being referred to pejoratively in absentia are significant barriers to dialogue. Despite the unprecedented nature and explicit goal of the Synod, it nonetheless listened *with exception*. It is my conviction that listening *without exception* is possible.

Through a lens shaped by the ubiquitous narrative of loss, Disaffiliating Catholics will never be seen as a source of insight and as potentially contributing something constructive to the faith. Affirmative theological reflection is rarely applied to those who have "Lapsed."

To understand better the complex experience of disaffiliation, to listen for insights from those who are experiencing or witnessing such disaffiliation, and to explore its implications for the church, education, and world, this book explores one "place" where the religiously-affiliated and religiously-disaffiliating regularly meet—Catholic secondary schools—and suggests something interesting is happening.

Like the synod of Catholic bishops, I agree that the lived experience and practices of young adults are one place the Divine makes itself known. So I suggest that the edge of religious affiliation is not a thin boundary separating something from nothing but a place filled with dynamic religious

2. See *Instrumentum Laboris*, 2018.

3. Asterisk added to treat the various names of our creator with the utmost respect, as in the Jewish tradition, and also to keep the name and its meaning open.

4. Disaffiliating Catholics have become a significant focus of the New Evangelization and a large-scale public relations campaign in the United States for disillusioned Catholics to "Stay With Us."

options. "Non-practicing Catholics," for example, practice something. What they practice, they learned. What they learned, they were taught. This "religiousness" that remains at the edge of religious affiliation is flowing in multiple directions and through boundaries that once distinguished who is religious from who is not. Moreover, it is not only the religious lives of disaffiliating young adults that reflect the new patterns of this space, but also the educators who teach them religion. So in a series of ethnographic portraits, I blend descriptive and analytic research to suggest that something good is happening in this current fluidity that many describe as a crisis.

A PORTRAIT PREVIEW

When I met with Michael, thirty-two-years-old, and his former theology teacher, Eliot, fifty-six-years-old,[5] I was curious how the pair would discuss the potentially uncomfortable topic of religious disaffiliation that had developed since their time together as teacher and student. Eliot had described Michael as one of the few students who seemed to understand what he was trying to do as a teacher, and who was willing to try on religious ideas not because they were going to be on the next test but because they might influence his everyday life.

Michael spoke positively of his Catholic childhood and his religious education, but no longer attends Mass regularly or participates in a parish. He works for a consulting firm and lives with his fiancée. They are not planning a Catholic wedding. Michael concedes he does not have "a good label" for who he is religiously, but he believes his religious education was successful.

Like Michael, his teacher Eliot grew up in a Catholic family and attended an all-boys Catholic high school. He earned advanced degrees in theology and explored a vocation as a priest. Eliot has now taught religion in Catholic high schools for over thirty years. Prior to this meeting with Michael, Eliot shared with me that he has always wanted to sit down with one of his former students to see what they remembered years later from his courses—"and hit 'em with a few more lessons." On a hot summer day

---

5. I have given each of the research participants pseudonyms to keep their identities confidential. All the proper names of places and people given during their interviews have similarly been changed. All interviews and observations were conducted in New York City between April and June of 2017.

Introduction

in New York City, on the day of his school's reunion, Eliot got that chance. But the lesson was (thankfully) more of an exchange.

Despite their differences, our conversation moved easily and with humor and reflection into the potentially tense questions at the core of this study. I was relieved and moved by the immediate and easy intergenerational banter between like-minded men who clearly enjoy talking about things that matter.

Michael shared thoughtfully with his former teacher of religion that Eliot's courses had helped guide him through the diverse religious worlds he encountered after he left high school. He discussed the comfort and capacity he had learned to "go outside of religion to find religious answers" and to "go outside of being Catholic to find spiritual answers" because his high school courses included an exchange between religious and nonreligious sources and concepts. Michael admitted that Eliot had probably never explicitly suggested leaving the Catholic Church to explore other religious identities and practices, but "I heard it" nonetheless, he explained.

Michael exemplifies the experience of a growing group of young Catholics who live in a diverse and fluid religious space. The religious learning that readied him for an educated departure from a conventionally-affiliated Catholic identity into that space is a significant experience for the fields of religious education and practical theology to explore. Why? For similar reasons that the conversation was challenging and insightful for Eliot. It asked him to wrestle with, rather than dismiss, the complexity of the religious life of Michael and others like him.

After listening to and speaking with Michael, Eliot agreed with him that this religious education experience had been successful. Michael had learned what Eliot had intended to convey. When I asked Eliot whether affiliation was important to him as a goal in his practice of teaching religion, he surprised us both with his response. "My gut says 'no.'"

Eliot's conclusion during and after these conversations was not the only one made by participating educators. After a similar conversation with her former disaffiliated student, I asked Theresa, another teacher with over thirty years of experience, whether she thought the religious educational experience had been successful. Her answer was also surprising, but unique. She twisted in her seat as she explained, "I don't know how to say 'yes,' but I can't say 'no' either."

Sitting with these teachers and learners as they shared their experiences, I was moved by the respect between them that was immediately apparent and that seemed to grow as the conversation progressed. The conversations included thoughtful humor about the irony of the religious results, discomfort with their conflicting views, and agreement on the importance of the questions they were exploring together in this study. All the research participants suggested that religious life and learning today couldn't be done responsibly without this wider dialogue including persons and communities who question particular truth claims and challenge expectations of affiliation. Together, affiliated teachers and disaffiliating learners also shared concern for what it means if connection to the tradition is completely lost. The encounters, replete with this vulnerability and anxiety, reveal that something interesting is happening in and at the edge of religious affiliation that is both creative and critical, and potentially good.

As I turned the corner after saying my goodbyes after the final interview with Michael and Eliot, I looked back to see that these two men, who on the surface appear quite different, had sat back down to continue their conversation. That image is my hope for this book. With that hope in mind, I invite you into these respectful dialogues to explore the questions: What is happening here? Is it working? Why?, and to encounter possibly challenging responses. The encounters between disaffiliating persons and their teachers of religion portrayed here suggest that listening without exception is possible and they reveal that existing theories need amendment to better understand the religious life and learning happening at the edge of religious affiliation.

chapter 1

LIKE WATER OR LIKE ROCK?

Religious Affiliation in Today's Context
of Education and Ministry

The sociologist Zygmunt Bauman describes contemporary more fluid cultural circumstances as "liquid modernity" rather than "late" or "post" modernity.¹ Despite the potentially positive elements of that term, Bauman's image takes a rather pessimistic but understandable view that more fluid, subjective, and syncretistic modes of living distort tradition and set individuals adrift. Other theorists suggest there is reason to embrace the fluidity of today.² This chapter explores just what is changing religiously in the United States, and focuses on the perceived decline of religion—particularly within the Catholic Church.

According to the Pew Research Center, in 2014, 23 percent of the US adult population has disaffiliated from their inherited religions and institutional communities.³ With each new study, these numbers increase.⁴

1. Bauman, *Liquid Modernity*.

2. Thomas Tweed uses liquid imagery to develop an overall theory of contemporary religion. His theory of religion is "above all, about movement and relation, and it is an attempt to correct theories that have presupposed stasis and minimized interdependence." Tweed defines religion itself as a confluence of cultural flows that intensify joy and confront suffering by drawing on human and suprahuman forces to make homes and cross boundaries. See Tweed, *Crossing and Dwelling*, 54, 77.

3. See Lipka, "Closer Look at America's Rapidly Growing Religious 'Nones.'"

4. During the writing of this chapter, the British Social Attitudes survey and the biennial European Social Survey conducted by Stephen Bullivant at St. Mary's University reported that religious disaffiliated person—also known as "nones"—now make up 48.6 percent of the British population. The study reports Anglicans account for 17.1 percent, Catholics 8.7 percent, other Christian denominations 17.2 percent and non-Christian

The 2016 PRRI study reports that fully one-quarter (25 percent) of North Americans claim no formal religious identity. This group is now the single largest "religious group" in the United States.[5] Catholicism in the United States has experienced the "greatest net losses" as a result of these changes in religious participation.[6] For a denomination canonically difficult to leave, a significant number of North American Catholics are leaving, or at least migrating beyond the institution's immediate influence.[7]

Disaffiliating Catholics now make up at least 10 percent of the overall adult US population. To put these statistics in context, only 17 percent of the population is Baptist; 24 percent are Catholic.[8] "Former" Catholics are the third-largest "religious group" in the United States.[9]

This somewhat cohesive movement influencing not just Catholicism but the whole of North American religion has real consequences for those invested in religious institutions. Three thousand five hundred churches close every year in the United States while just one thousand new churches open.[10] Moreover, recent studies show the movement now extends beyond the mostly male (57 percent) and white (68 percent) group that is has been. Disaffiliating persons are the fastest growing subgroup among Latinx communities.[11] These changes in conventional religious participation are happening across many denominations, all groups, and at all levels.[12] Current research also reports that contrary to lifespan patterns of increased religious affiliation as persons grow older, marry and have children among earlier generations; generational cohorts are now becoming

---

religions 8.4 percent. See Sherwood, "Nearly 50% Are of No Religion."

5. Cooper et al., "Exodus: Why Americans Are Leaving Religion."

6. Although roughly the same amount of United States residents identify as Catholic today as in the 1970s, the effects of migration obscure the larger trend of movement out from standard affiliation with the Roman Catholic Church in the United States. See Murphy, "Half of U.S. Adults Raised Catholic."

7. According to Pew, 52 percent of all adults who were raised Catholic have left the church at some point in their lives. Moreover, recent research suggests that Catholic schooling has little or no effect on maintaining conventional Catholic affiliation later in life. See Perl and Grey, "Catholic Schooling and Disaffiliation from Catholicism."

8. Liu, "'Nones' on the Rise."

9. Murphy, "Half of U.S. Adults Raised Catholic Have Left the Church."

10. Anderson et al., "Dearly Departed."

11. Impertori, *Cuéntame*; Paulson, "Even as U.S. Hispanics Lift Catholicism."

12. Monitoring email list serves and online activity I have seen more and more organizations like "African Americans for Humanism" or "The Black Skeptics of Los Angeles."

less religiously affiliated with age.[13] All that said, the experience of disaffiliation is still not well understood.

In order to situate the portraits of the next chapters in this dynamic context and better understand the persons portrayed, this chapter details three aspects of contemporary changing religious patterns: (1) the multiplicity of options (2), "The Rise of the Nones"—and "Somes,"[14] and (3) a remix religious style shared among both "Nones" and "Somes."

LIKE WATER

Religion or being religious is not, and has never been, a single thing. It is a complex pattern of human culture and behavior. It is an active way of being that images an ultimate reality in response to the life that surrounds us. Religion and religiousness then refer to a personal experience that is lived, and to a social experience that is shared concerning what a person most values, depends on, and considers sacred. Thomas Tweed helpfully suggests that religions are confluences of "organic-cultural flows" that shape meaning, amplify joy, and contend with suffering in everyday life. These flows emerge from the sources, symbols, and stories available to give life meaning. With these materials, persons make both homes in which to dwell and vehicles with which to cross boundaries to other shores.[15] Doing, being, and practicing religion is always a learned and unique interpretive mixture responding to experiences of the individual.[16]

Thus, to respond to the question "What does it mean to be religious today?" we need a definition fluid enough to incorporate the reality of more sources, symbols, and stories available to persons today.

LIQUID MODERNITY

Scholars across disciplines note the existence of meaning frames and cultural circumstances that function as the non-conscious conditions for

---

13. Lipka, "Millennials Increasingly Are Driving Growth of 'Nones.'"
14. Drescher offers the opposing term "Some" to juxtapose with the unaffiliated "Nones." I pick up the term for this reason and also, as she mentions, the "Somes" represent a dynamic contemporary phenomenon of religious choices and remixing. See Drescher, *Choosing Our Religion*.
15. Tweed, *Crossing and Dwelling*, 54.
16. Schmidt-Leukel, *Transformation by Integration*, 58.

all production of knowledge and belief. These conditions and narratives operate historically in distinct and specific periods. These institutions, discourses, and social propositions regulate human thought and behavior and form the epistemological assumptions that shape shared understandings of self, others, and the world. Charles Taylor's book *A Secular Age* details the evolution of what he calls the Western cultural "social imaginary" as an intuitional background that conditions all perspectives—particularly of how a people create meaning. These conditions of belief have developed, says Taylor, from an understanding of the self as immersed in an enchanted cosmos to the contemporary more "immanent" but "cross-pressured" frame in which people feel competing pressures to both believe and doubt.[17] These distinct cultural circumstances of historical periods teach something more than mere behavior, mastery of information, or specific skills. They form the organizing principle a people bring to thinking, feeling, and relating to others and themselves.[18] This cultural curriculum invariably also forms and informs religious beliefs and practices.

While Bauman and Taylor agree on the function of such forces in society, they appraise them differently. Bauman is pessimistic. Taylor is optimistic. Robert Kegan's developmental view of the changing epistemic expectations of such a cultural curriculum is helpful here. He proposes that these social imaginaries or the epistemological systems within which people live, move, and make their meaning develop, just as individuals do.[19] These culturally formed ways of knowing undergo fundamental transformations as more and more persons no longer take them for granted. This is how we "get somewhere religiously."[20] If all goes well, says Kegan, there is progress toward more humane historical stages by enfolding previous ways of thinking into more inclusive and complex ways of knowing.[21] This more fluid progression is the point on which this conversation now turns. We have long taken for granted fixed religious norms and affiliation to boundaried communities. But those are now being contested.

---

17. Taylor, *Secular Age*.
18. Kegan, *In Over Our Heads*, 217.
19. Kegan, *In Over Our Heads*, 217.
20. Nagle, "How We Get Somewhere Religiously."
21. Kegan, *In Over Our Heads*.

LIKE WATER OR LIKE ROCK?

DISAFFILIATION IN LIQUID MODERNITY

In 1948, 91 percent of North Americans identified as Christian and 73 percent were affiliated church members.[22] The United States remains a predominantly Christian nation, but that dominance is showing signs of change. Today, 70 percent of adults identify as Christian.[23] And although the majority still attends church regularly, the percentage of affiliated church members dropped to 60 percent in the 2000s. When Gallup and Pew Research surveyed North Americans in 2014 about their belief in G*d, this number had dropped from 98 percent in 1966 to a still considerable 86 percent. But that number slips further to 80 percent among young adults born between 1990 and 1996.[24] To add both more complexity and clarity to what might be changing, a 2018 study found that 90 percent believe in a higher power, but only a slim majority believes in the G*d described by Christian churches.[25]

Recent research on Catholic Church members and their behavior reveals similar trends. The Official Catholic Directory that records each parishioner in the United States who attends Mass, receives a sacrament, or donates, has 68.1 million on its rolls. There is an interesting gap between that number and the 81 million North Americans who identify themselves as Catholics in some way.[26] Only about one in three self-identified Catholics (31.4 percent) attend Mass in any given week.[27] And young people today are not returning to affiliated religious status as they get older, marry, and have families.[28] Findings like these suggest that adherence to fixed norms and boundaries as a defining quality of religion is now contested in everyday life. What these statistics do not capture that Bauman's image of "liquid modernity" does is that the contemporary cultural circumstances involve a new norm of fluidity in just about every sector of human life—whether in jobs, or racial, ethnic, and religious diversity.

These are important demographic and cultural currents. But current events like the 2016 election reveal a corresponding reactive retrenchment

22. Newport, "Questions and Answers about Americans' Religion."
23. Wormald, "Religious Landscape Study."
24. Lipka, "Millennials Increasingly Are Driving Growth of 'Nones.'"
25. Lipka and Gecewicz, "More Americans Now Say They're Spiritual but Not Religious."
26. Grossmann, "How Catholic Are US Catholics?"
27. CARA, "Sacraments Today."
28. Liu, "Religious Switching and Intermarriage."

by white, working-class, Christian (and Catholic) men (and some women) who perceive the blurring of boundaries and change as a threat. The political influence of this voting block is now undeniable. This group feels that the new cultural curriculum has left them behind, or as Kegan would say, leaves them "In Over Their Heads."[29]

Despite the 2016 election, Pew reports that the majority say increasing diversity makes the United States a better place to live.[30] Although the rhetoric of the 2016 election divided the population, Pew's American Trends survey finds that North Americans express more positive feelings toward differing religious groups today than they did just a few years ago.[31]

Clearly, the contemporary religious context is complex. The Pew data and the cultural backlash so influential in the last election demonstrate both the taken-for-granted-ness of certain long-held social and religious assumptions, and how changes to those norms are being contested. One example of this is that North Americans today do not inherit religion like they used to. Between 34 and 42 percent of adults currently have a religious identity different from the one in which they were raised.[32]

In his book *Religion and Public Life: A Dilemma for Democracy*, Ronald Thieman suggests that the "Lively American Experiment"[33] of individual mobility, freedom of choice, and non-establishment and free exercise of religion would inevitably lead to a multiculturalism and religious pluralism that its constituents might not be able to handle—at first.[34] This contemporary experience in the United States corresponds to an overall globalization that has accelerated the rate of change in all areas of human activity. Even Bauman admits two things about liquid modernity: that (1) there is no

---

29. Kegan, *In Over Our Heads*.

30. Cohn and Caumont, "10 Demographic Trends."

31. People in all the major religious groups, by Democrats and Republicans, men and women, and younger and older adults express the increase in more affirming feelings. According to the Pew study, only two of the groups analyzed give another group a lower rating than in 2014. And the feelings are mutual. Despite what you may have guessed, it is not Republicans and Muslims. Atheists rate their feelings toward evangelical Christians lower than they did in 2014. White evangelical Protestants also rate their feelings toward Atheists lower than in 2014. See Mitchell, "Americans Express Increasingly Warm Feelings toward Religious Groups."

32. Wormald, "Religious Landscape Study."

33. See Sidney Meade's oft-cited historical work *The Lively Experiment: The Shaping of Christianity in America*, which traces the creative tensions and strange alliances formed during the development of religious freedom and democracy in the young United States.

34. Thiemann, *Religion in Public Life*.

going back; and that (2) social institutions lag behind the pace and diversity of everyday experience. Harold Horell adds that this fluid reality has encouraged the melting of modern foundationalism and of those institutions' reliance on provided metanarratives for meaning and purpose[35]—especially for those who were marginalized by them. In this context, the dramatic response to the survey question "What is your religious affiliation?" reveals more about once dominant religious expectations in the United States than it does about those who give the answer "None."[36]

There is indeed a deinstitutionalization of religion and a mounting defense of conventional borders. But despite associated fears, it appears that something interesting is happening as more and more people live and move in-between the disputed boundary of "affiliated" and "disaffiliated." What is happening in this place filled by the many fissures from old religious containers does not indicate religious decline but marks of emerging religious currents. For example, although some suggest that religion in the United States is drying up according to conventional measures of religious affiliation, the number of people who say they experience a deep sense of spirituality is *rising*.[37] The next section explores where that sense of spirituality, or religiousness, is going if not to Mass, synagogue, or mosque.

AN EXPLOSION OF OPTIONS

One cannot ignore the remarkable number of religious possibilities in the United States. Taylor argues that we are living in a religious supernova, a kind of "galloping pluralism" as institutions run out of both fuel and influence. The conditions of which began with the social imaginary that Taylor calls the "immanent frame."[38] Starting in early modernity, cultural circumstances taught that the world was made up of what Taylor calls "buffered

---

35. Bauman, *Liquid Modernity*, 83.

36. Ramey and Miller, "Meaningless Surveys."

37. Masci and Lipka, "Americans May Be Getting Less Religious, but Feelings of Spirituality Are on the Rise." This linguistic dualism of spiritual and religious can obscure more than it reveals, but I contend that they belong in the same ecology or ecosystem. Whatever religion and spirituality are today, they inhabit this more fluid space together where the burden of meaning construction has been transferred from institutions to individuals. People in America today, both religiously affiliated and disaffiliating, are choosing their meaning system rather than inheriting it. See Drescher, *Choosing Our Religion*, 7.

38. Taylor, *Secular Age*, 300.

individuals" protected by ritual and social practices from supernatural beings or forces that were now thought to be delusions.[39] In an immanent world, humans construct order and meaning. This did not spell the end of transcendence, however.

Taylor argues that persons today feel "cross pressured" by the pluralism they encounter. They are pushed by immanence and also pulled by a desire to seek human fullness beyond the immanent frame.[40] Transcendence persists in an enduring "sense of our deep nature, of a current running through all things, which also resonates in us; the experience of being opened up to something deeper and fuller by contact with nature; the sense of an intra-cosmic mystery."[41] He points to the Franciscans, Protestants, Spiritualists, and Humanists to suggest there has always been some form of dissatisfaction with closed world structures.[42]

Taylor's work presents a historical-philosophical view of the larger religious context and what religious disaffiliation might represent. The through-line connecting Taylor and the other cultural and religious observers engaged thus far is their description of a contemporary space created where people can move in and around, and cross once consequential boundaries in order to believe and practice "otherwise."[43] The theorists to follow will do more of the work describing this new normal where Christians are raised to contest truth claims, taught to value discovery, and formed in self-expression. In this context, it is reasonable to ask: How might religiousness be expressed in ways other than affiliation?

THE RISE OF THE NONES—AND SOMES

The "Nones"—the religiously disaffiliating or unaffiliated—have been a small minority throughout the history of the United States, but the Pew and Trinity College surveys of the 1990s attracted new curiosity and worry when they reported that their number increased from 7.1 percent to 15.3 percent from the 1980s to the 2000s. A total of twenty-five million people left the religions of their families, or new faiths to which they had

---

39. Taylor, *Secular Age*, 539.
40. Taylor, *Secular Age*, 302.
41. Taylor, *Secular Age*, 350.
42. Taylor, *Secular Age*, 351.
43. Taylor, *Secular Age*, 257.

converted.⁴⁴ In 2012, 20 percent of adults claimed no religious affiliation. By 2016, unaffiliated adults represented 25 percent of the population.⁴⁵ The Pew Center had projected disaffiliation increasing to 26 percent of the population, but not until 2050.⁴⁶

These statistics reveal a contemporary story. Nearly one in five North American adults was raised in a religion before disaffiliating from it. Only 4 percent have moved in the other direction.⁴⁷ In other words, for every person who has converted, more than four people have de-converted. These studies also reveal that (1) very few Nones just drift away;⁴⁸ and (2) Nones are not that different from many religious affiliates.

Elizabeth Drescher suggests the provocative pairing of "Somes" to the phenomenon and category of "None." She intends the term to describe the religiously affiliated, but the language, as well has her findings, imply that Nones and Somes are not opposites. "Somes" are not "Tons" or "Totally Ins," so to speak. They have some affiliation to a particular religion, and some other stuff too. Drescher paints a poignant image of this shared quality of Somes and Nones: half empty church parking lots on Sunday mornings as both religiously affiliated and disaffiliating persons drive by on their way to hiking, surfing, dog parks, and brunch to enjoy intimacy with friends and/or the natural world.⁴⁹ While the majority of North Americans still believe in G*d, pray regularly, and think religion is a positive force, more and more are making different religious choices—choices that are not being measured by church attendance surveys.

The practical theologian Tom Beaudoin suggests that the choice to drive by that church parking lot on Sunday morning, and claiming "None" as an identity, are part of a new experience and new space in and from which to manage the fluidity of today. Like Catholics who qualify their level of adherence, the term "None" provides a language to qualify the

---

44. Downey, "Religious Affiliation, Education and Internet Use."

45. Cooper et al., "Exodus."

46. Drescher, *Choosing Our Religion*, 6.

47. Liu, "Global Religious Landscape."

48. One particular and focused example of this research comes from an "exit interview" survey of nearly three hundred "lapsed" Catholics in Trenton, NJ, in 2011. Byron and Zech demonstrated that an overwhelming number of their respondents shared that they had left the Church, but a quarter still considered themselves Catholic. They cited the failure of the institution and clerics as their reason for leaving the Church but not the tradition. See Byron and Zech, "On Their Way Out."

49. Drescher, *Choosing Our Religion*, 247.

provisional quality of religion in the current context and therefore should imply a mix of something, not a lack.[50]

As the portraits in the following chapters suggest, affiliated religious identities (Somes) are no less dynamic and complex. Affiliated religiousness appears to "harbor elements of disaffiliation, and vice versa."[51] In other words, both are living and learning religiously in liquid modernity. The explosion of religious alternatives represents one factor catalyzing the fluidity of religious identity for both Somes and Nones.

The chemical term "catalyst" offers a helpful metaphor here as it refers to a substance that increases the rate change with much less energy.[52] Due to religious alternatives and other catalyzing factors, scholars predict that the fluidity of religious identities will continue to increase steadily driven by the emerging generation who encounter each other and mix with much less effort than was needed in the past, and who value mobility, difference, choice, and change.

Millennials, young adults born after 1980, have likely surpassed Baby Boomers (born 1946–1964) as the largest generation in the United States and differ significantly from their elders. They are the most racially diverse generation in the country's history: 43 percent of Millennial adults are non-white. They are likely to be the most educated generation to date, and are the most religiously unaffiliated generation in history.[53] New media practices, among other things, have changed how they see difference, express difference, and participate in relationships with religiously diverse others. Millennials have learned to appreciate difference in many areas of their lives and for them difference is less a distinguishing barrier than an invitation to engagement.[54] Whether or not there are boundaries anymore is a fair question given that same-sex marriage and nonbinary gender identities are part of the national discourse.

This pluralism and the religious options now available have always existed. North American Christians have always had Jews as neighbors.

---

50. I am grateful to Tom Beaudoin for many conversations and guidance regarding this work. The quotations here reflect follow-up and comments on his response to Elizabeth Drescher presented at Fordham University in 2016.

51. Beaudoin, "Response to Elizabeth Drescher's 'Cosmopolitan Christianities.'"

52. Helmenstine, "What Does a Catalyst Do in a Chemical Reaction?"

53. See Grant, "Analysis: 7.5 Million Americans Lost Their Religion since 2012"; Liu, "Religion among the Millennials"; Lipka, "Millennials Increasingly Are Driving Growth of 'Nones.'"

54. Drescher, *Choosing Our Religion*, 61.

Buddhists, Muslims, and Atheists did not just suddenly appear. Strong institutions made choosing such religious options—even relationships—unviable for earlier generations. As long as such alternative worldviews were located on the other side of the world or town, they were characterized as too incomprehensible, perhaps even despised, to adopt.[55]

What has changed in the last sixty years is that the previously unquestioned institutions and their powerful claims on people have lost their grip, in part because varied practices and beliefs have become so familiar. Taylor refers to this new proximity, which makes religious choices and the rejection of certain old views more accessible and acceptable, as "fragilization."[56] Otherness—including religious otherness—is no longer on the other side of the world or town, but on the other side of the bed.

People married since 2000 are about twice more likely to be in religious intermarriages than were people who got married before 1960. Nearly four in ten married people who were wed since 2010 have a spouse who identifies with a different religious group.[57] Interfaith relationships are even more common among unmarried people who are living together, 49 percent of whom have a partner with a different religion. Despite institutional discouragement, the rate of intermarriage continues to increase.[58] Mixed-faith relationships are becoming more common driven in large part by marriages between Christians and—Nones. Pew reports that 18 percent of North Americans who have gotten married since 2010 are either Christians with a religiously disaffiliated spouse or "Nones" with a Christian spouse. By comparison, just 5 percent of people surveyed who got married before 1960 fit this profile.[59]

Drescher suggests that we need a new verb to describe what is happening. She offers "the Noneing of American Religion" to describe the collective process of deinstitutionalization and pluralization.[60] This attempt is lacking for a number of reasons. First, it is clunky. Second, it continues to imply a lack of something "religious" while research suggests that there is no such lack. She is correct, however, that there is a need for a new lens.

---

55. Taylor, *Secular Age*, 304.
56. Taylor, *Secular Age*, 303–4.
57. Liu, "Global Religious Landscape."
58. Katz-Miller, *Being Both*, xiii.
59. Liu, "Global Religious Landscape."
60. Drescher, *Choosing Our Religion*.

Drescher's other neologism of "Somes" to pair with Nones, successfully conveys the catalyzing and mixing that "Noneing" does not.

Despite the negativism of the language, Drescher and Taylor argue that the resulting faith from Noneing and fragilization is not necessarily a weakened faith. Data suggests that disaffiliating North Americans are neither more nor less religious than their affiliated counterparts when religiousness is understood beyond the narrow view of affiliation associated with demographic research. Drescher argues there is a common and shared desire among both Somes and Nones for a more fluid identity of growth and change throughout their lives.[61] This appears to be an important element of contemporary religiousness.

Drescher's national qualitative study adds a number of qualities that define that desire and the practices of Nones and many Somes. The emerging religiousness in the United States: (1) is embedded in everyday life and locations rather than in separate sacred spaces and during sacred times; (2) is embodied, sensate, and social as opposed to mainly private and internalized self-empowerment; (3) is relational rather than institutional; (4) is provisional and fluid, reflecting new experiences and resources while remaining coherent within personal narratives; (5) is understood as both personally and socially transformative; (6) highlights the experience of authenticity and connectedness in the present moment rather than a future-oriented expectation of salvation or reward.[62] The portraits presented in the following chapters resonate with this analysis of remixing rather than losing religion.

REMIXING RELIGION

The once consequential boundaries of religious affiliation and difference have become porous to create a fluid space where bodies move and mix. The confluence of religious pluralism found in this space plays an important part in the ability to believe and practice otherwise.[63] Interfaith families,

---

61. Drescher, *Choosing Our Religion*, 31–33.

62. Drescher, *Choosing Our Religion*, 119.

63. The vastly expanded contemporary social media also provides immediate and relational access to diverse details of everyday religious life and the people living it. Drescher suggests that technology in particular undermines the structural expectation of affiliation. The logic of digitally integrated social practices encourage self-representation in which affiliational commitments are muted. The expression of religious and spiritual perspectives signal a lack of institutional, doctrinal rigidity. See Drescher, *Choosing Our*

for example, are growing in number, and are raising children in a blended style of two or more religious traditions. The idea of being both, however, presents a challenge to notions of exclusive religious identity and affiliation. A stronger case may be made that it offers a helpful new view in a world where interfaith friendship, love, and marriage are increasingly common and inevitable remixed realities.

Remix studies scholars define remix as a contemporary practice enabled by the convergence of various technologies, and the increased exposure and access to ever-expanding sources of cultural content.[64] Despite understandable resistance to this practice when it comes to religion, Peter van der Veer argues that every religion is "sampled,"[65] remixed, and syncretistic—so much so that it is often impossible for historians to decipher which elements have come from where.[66] What seems clear to remix scholars is that in the twenty-first century, all interpretation of contemporary cultural forms will have to engage with questions of remix, modularity, and mobility.[67] Religious symbols and practices in particular are increasingly being dis-embedded and repurposed from their original traditions.

Religions have become symbolic "tool-boxes" from which men and women today draw freely, without necessarily identifying themselves with the bounded tradition or institution from which the symbol came.[68] With this remixing, it is important to remember that the traditionalist idea that "we have always done it this way" is never really true.

Many religious traditions, including Catholicism, developed through such processes, integrating elements from various cultural and religious sources. Some people suggest that the most important moments in Christian history occurred when Christianity "rubbed up against" the world and integrated elements learned from extra-ecclesial sources, resulting in a richer and more empowering tradition.[69] Despite the orderly quality and

---

Religion, 11, 62.

64. See Navas et al., *Routledge Companion to Remix Studies*, 8.

65. The term "sampling" comes from the common remix practices of hip-hop artists from the art form's inception. The *Urban Dictionary* defines the term as the process of taking short segments of sound from a song, movie, or elsewhere and using that collage of sounds to form a musical piece. *Urban Dictionary*, s.v. "sampling," http://www.urbandictionary.com/define.php?term=sampling.

66. Schmidt-Leukel, *Transformation by Integration*, 67.

67. See Navas, *Remix Theory*.

68. Beaudoin, *Virtual Faith*, 148.

69. Some examples of this would be early Christianity's relationship with Judaism,

attempts of institutions to resist the flow of time and neutralize its effects, more fluid—living!—forces have always slowly shaped and reshaped rock-like religious-cultural norms. And according to Pelikan, the resistance to that process is what gives tradition a bad name.[70] Although the critique that this will lead to complete relativism may be understandable, there has never been a unanimous, homogenous, or fixed Christianity.

Blending of religion with other ideologies can also be damaging, as it is when values are bent to serve right wing, nationalist, and racial politics. That said, the religiousness of liquid modernity is not just a fluid chaos. Research suggests it is flowing in some directions but not others.

Moreover, like the traditioning process shaping and reshaping religion, this remix style both deconstructs and reconstructs conventional religious practices, doctrines, morals, and authority in an ongoing "trialectic" between the culture, tradition, and the experience of individuals immersed in them both.[71] Perhaps this is what is most significant in the apparent decline of religion but increase in spirituality. As the personal experience of North Americans increasingly exposes them to multiple religious traditions and secular worldviews, individuals have no choice but to integrate the truth, goodness, and holiness they encounter in other worldviews and persons who hold them. The theologian Perry Schmidt-Leukel argues that this is precisely the expectation of conversion in conventional models of evangelization. Missionaries value the religious mobility and choice of the convert—as long as they choose Christianity.[72] Schmidt-Leukel adds that the exposure and choice to integrate the good encountered in other worldviews also includes becoming critically aware of the good that has not yet been realized within one's own religion.[73]

Scholasticism, and Greek philosophy, and Vatican II with social sciences and the modern world. Rabbi Irwin Kula from the National Jewish Center for Learning and Leadership in New York City used this physical image of "rubbing up against" to suggest that many major religious traditions have developed through processes of syncretism, reform, and remixing. His remarks were part of a forum at Fordham University, Lincoln Center, February 10, 2016.

70. Pelikan, *Vindication of Tradition*.

71. The significance and process involving an ongoing trialectic shares some similarity with James and Evelyn Whitehead's approach to theological reflection engaging the various sources of religious information (culture, tradition, and experience) to make pastoral decisions and take action. See Whitehead, *Method in Ministry*.

72. Schmidt-Leukel, *Transformation by Integration*, 7.

73. Schmidt-Leukel, *Transformation by Integration*, 7.

Similarly today both Somes and Nones are realizing the limitations of conventional communities by learning in the presence of different persons and diverse religious options. Persons now remix meaning systems from available religious and secular symbols, texts, and moral codes. Even single-faith families and traditional religious communities have absorbed this religious style.[74] The phenomenon of religious Sisters practicing and teaching Reiki, for example, and Jesuits combining the Ignatian Exercises with yoga for what they call "Chapel Yoga," enlarges and clarifies the Christian tradition for many.

According to Drescher, these expressions by "Somes," although religiously affiliated, demonstrate discomfort with fixed identity markers and preference for more provisional and experimental choices of religious status.[75] While they may start with the traditional religious identity as a base, Somes are growing more comfortable with tempering problematic elements by drawing from and remixing with other traditions, practices, and experiences they see as more authentic.

This increasingly normative dynamic religious culture that mixes elements at the level of lived religion to create new form and content reflects the sense of tradition learned and expressed by an individual living and interpreting it rather than responding to the dictates of authorities. The supposed unanimous testimony of a homogenous tradition has never existed.[76] Religiousness is always unmistakably interpreted and lived as a unique mixture.[77]

In today's more fluid context, this question of continuity with tradition and religiousness has been reshaped into a question of authenticity.[78] Many critics view these trends of choice, mobility, and remixing as overly individualistic rejections of tradition. The next section explores some of these criticisms.

---

74. Drescher, *Choosing Our Religion*, 9.
75. Drescher, *Choosing Our Religion*, 34.
76. Pelikan, *Vindication of Tradition*.
77. Schmidt-Leukel, *Transformation by Integration*, 58.
78. The idea and term of "Catholicness" or "Jewishness" represents this fluid and subjective quality of religious identity in common conversation and life. While I hear these terms often in conversation, what they mean differs from person to person.

REVIEW OF THE CONTEMPORARY CRITIQUE

The US context has granted and immersed people in the unprecedented freedom to experiment with worldviews and practices, and the ability to try on numerous identities. Yet discussing religion in this liquid modernity cannot be done without situating that effort in the contested discourse surrounding it.

Bauman articulates a common element of the critique when he argues that liquid modernity and its desire for authenticity have shaped the course of life into a series of self-focused and self-referential pursuits.[79] J. K. Smith, a Reformed Christian theologian, similarly suggests that this intoxicating expressive individualism "is just in the water."[80] Bauman argues that this freedom and focus on authenticity creates a gap between self-assertion and the capacity for self-control that sentences individuals to lifetimes of solitary confinement.[81]

Robert Bellah's introduction of Sheila, and her personal religion, "Sheilism," remains an important example for those who critique contemporary subjectivity.[82] Many scholars of a variety of disciplines have suggested that this individualism is incompatible with community and rejects religious tradition. Although this search for the authentic or true self resonates with elements of established Christian traditions, observers like Bauman and Christian Smith view this resonance as an unfortunate confluence that adulterates faith and sends many on a fool's adventure of self-discovery that has no end.[83] The individual selection of values and practices associated with "Sheilaism," Bauman argues, suggests to religious learners that meaning is to be lived here and now rather than as a future goal to be lived toward.[84]

Robert Putnam's well-known book *Bowling Alone* argues that the rising disaffiliation and decline in traditional communities is the result of a wide and pervasive culture of disconnection and anti-institutionalism.[85] Christian Smith's significant *National Study of Youth and Religion* (NSYR)

---

79. Bauman, *Liquid Modernity*, 311.
80. J. K. Smith, *How (Not) to Be Secular*, 12.
81. Bauman, *Liquid Modernity*, 37.
82. Bellah et al., *Individualism & Commitment in American Life*.
83. Bauman, *Liquid Modernity*, 310; Smith and Lundquist, *Soul Searching*.
84. Bauman, *Liquid Modernity*, 310.
85. Putnam, *Bowling Alone*.

sounded a similar alarm—that the Christianity of young people today was no longer Christianity at all, but an individualistic "imposter" version that Smith and Melinda Denton call "Moral Therapeutic Deism."[86] Bauman adds to this value criticism an educational dimension by arguing that contemporary circumstances have collapsed learning into short term propositions that do not cohere into concepts like development or maturation required in tradition.[87] Using Gregory Bateson, he argues that the deconstructive learning valued today makes learners into "plankton" who "are unable to adhere to anything but the tide."[88] I think it is important to note the significance placed on adherence in Bauman's criticism.

Those critical of contemporary fluidity have launched countermeasures, such as the "New Evangelization," and the mandated curriculum in Catholic high schools[89] to try to get Nones and Somes to re-adhere. It has become a ministry "cottage industry."[90] Despite the attention, these ecclesial responses have produced nothing new. The New Evangelization, for example, has simply repackaged and restated old norms and leaves little room for the movement of the Spirit in the world. These countermeasures reflect a way of governing or sustaining authority rather than a way of educating.[91] Learners are moving on to other teachers because of it.[92]

86. Smith and Lundquist, *Soul Searching*, 162–70.

87. Bauman, *Liquid Modernity*, 304.

88. Bauman, *Liquid Modernity*, 312.

89. The "Doctrinal Elements of a Curriculum Framework for the Development of Catechetical Materials for Young People of High School Age," implemented by the United States Council of Catholic Bishops, is more commonly known by the name "The Bishop's Framework." The Catholic bishops of the United States unanimously approved and promulgated a mandated curriculum for Catholic high schools in 2008. The Bishop's Framework is the first time that the bishops sought to establish a uniform religious studies curriculum for all US Catholic secondary schools. The reception has been mixed, to say the least. The educators in this study, for example, refer to having to breathe life into a dead curriculum.

90. Drescher, *Choosing Our Religion*, 8.

91. Nicholas Lash argues that the office of "teachership" known as the magisterium has grown dangerously forgetful of this scriptural ideal and has substituted governance for education. Mature religious identity requires finding our place in an ongoing and diverse conversation. Lash suggests that the role of educators, and in particular bishops, is to act as moderators for this ongoing mature conversation. See Lash, "Teaching or Commanding."

92. Carrie Schroder at the University of San Francisco similarly found through her participatory action research of the Bishops' Framework in contemporary Catholic secondary schools that the new mandated curriculum significantly altered the content

Those justifying efforts like the New Evangelization and the Bishop's Framework may resonate with Taylor's description of the modern immanent frame, but they do not share his optimism that citizens of liquid modernity learn from the pluralism they encounter.[93] For Taylor, contemporary culture pushes in both directions, toward doubt and belief. In contrast, conventional criticism suggests that anything outside the established boundaries of religions' existent forms is *a priori* a rejection of both community and tradition. Whether or not this is an accurate analysis is at the heart of the contested conversation surrounding contemporary religious patterns. The constellating pessimistic views of some social scientists and theologians resemble what Taylor refers to as modern subtraction theories of secularization, in that they assume religion is in decline.[94] This reductive account of reality, he argues, so saturates the academy and ecclesial ministry that those who accept it are unable to imagine that religion is still a true motivator in people's lives when it is occurring outside traditional practices and in less familiar forms.[95] Research suggests that contemporary searches for authenticity in religious practices and commitments is not necessarily an overly individualistic pursuit. This and other studies find that both Somes and Nones make relational commitments where they feel they belong. Contrary to the critique, for them authenticity itself is a relational concept.

Religious studies scholar Courtney Bender argues that researchers can no longer assert that those practicing the more fluid religiousness of today are overly individualistic, unorganized, or untraditional. To do so reinforces problematic and prohibitive logics that simply cannot be objectively claimed as truth.[96] Bender found in her fieldwork that although contemporary religiousness does primarily involve personal experience, the lived worlds of participants are shaped more through ongoing, daily

---

students learn in religious studies courses and made demands on teachers to promote detailed doctrinal content in more teacher-centered modes of teaching and more conventional means of assessment. In so doing, teachers have had to stop or hide pre-Framework teaching practices that had been effective. Schroeder finds that the Bishops' Framework both lacks awareness of the present reality in Catholic secondary schools and presents the very real risk of diminishing students' interest in Catholic Tradition. See Schroeder, "U.S. Conference of Catholic Bishops' Doctrinal Elements of a Curriculum."

93. Taylor, *Secular Age*, 556.
94. Taylor, *Secular Age*.
95. Taylor, *Secular Age*, 433, 452–53.
96. Bender, *New Metaphysicals*, 182.

engagement in relational practices that afford authenticity and authority in their own bodies and attune them to the divine, and is not the product of aimless, disconnected individuals.[97] The anthropologist Abby Day similarly observes that what drives this is that contemporary religiousness is no longer only a propositional phenomenon.[98] In such a context, Beaudoin suggests our fields are diminished by our inability to think through how our basic categories "are caught up in past power relationships to which we no longer need to be subject."[99]

A COUNTER-CRITIQUE

There is a serious conversation to be had regarding the changing religious habits in the United States, but to do so will involve critical reflection. The weakness of more pessimistic views is that despite the reflexive turn in cultural studies that notes that any theorist's personal location, social status, and professional community shape all theoretical work, there is a tendency to affirm the notion that an omnispective view of a fixed religious terrain is possible—or that a religious authority can objectively decide what is and is not an authentic expression of religious belief and practice.[100] Moreover, the position can be uncritical of the powerful bias associated with this blind spot. This contested conversation surrounding changing religious norms and disaffiliation therefore involves negotiations of power, not just meaning.

Scholars have written on the problematic hegemonic history and present Western practice of defining religion and being religious. Paul Hedges refers to this problematic as "the World Religions Paradigm."[101] Fletcher describes a "container theory of religion."[102] And Boyarin has referred to the perpetuation of "Christianicity."[103] All of these critical perspectives suggest that this paradigm developed in Europe during the Reformation and colonial expansion now limits our understanding of religious identity and practice in varied contexts because it assumes: (1) that religions are

---

97. Bender, *New Metaphysicals*, 57.
98. Day, *Believing in Belonging*, 194.
99. Beaudoin, *Witness to Dispossession*, 68.
100. Tweed, *Crossing and Dwelling*, 27.
101. Hedges, "Multiple Religious Belonging after Religion."
102. Fletcher, "Religious Pluralism in an Era of Globalization."
103. Boyarin, *Border Lines*.

bounded territories of belonging; (2) that being religious means belonging to a bound territory based on adherence to a set of beliefs; (3) that these bounded territories of religion are internally regulated and consistent, and that therefore one cannot belong to more than one.[104]

This affiliation bias represents not only a sociological assumption but also a theologically derived logic of consensus and desire for order over against multiplicity and reform.[105] From this starting point, the corresponding pedagogy and evangelization becomes rooted theologically and practically in an exclusive and fixed relationship with an institution rather than in ongoing revelation. I refer to this hegemonic as a theology of affiliation.[106] It assumes that separated affiliated religious identities are the norm and the only legitimate possibility.

Moreover, the theology of affiliation and its assumptions of fixed borders fail when reviewing Christianity's own origins. For the church's first four hundred years, despite the myth of "parting ways," scholars still cannot clearly identify persons and practices as Christian or Jewish. The boundary between these two traditions was porous. Many people lived in the space in-between in some hybrid form. Similarly, dismissing the current cultural conditions and hybrid unaffiliated forms of practice that violate the theology of affiliation confines contemporary understanding and discourse on religiousness to domains defined by affiliation at a time when more and more people are instead living in spaces in-between. If practical theologians and religious educators want to remain credible and relevant, we need to reflect critically on this bias in our fields.

The theology of affiliation that dominates this contested conversation involves issues of power because it forms the ideological background against which and through which groups and persons are marginalized. Such discourse sets the rules that determine social, moral, and religious values. The work of Foucault, Gramsci, and others has revealed that power flows through institutional apparatuses and the discourse they create by defining the acceptable world of identity and relationships. These categories and sanctioned practices are often simply taken for granted, or seen as fixed and given. But

---

104. Hedges, "Multiple Religious Belonging after Religion."

105. Mathew Scruggs has written and presented on this bias in theology as another example of Whiteness that must be disrupted in light of diverse voices finally being heard in the academy. See Scruggs, "Symbolic Performativity."

106. Nagle, "How We Get Somewhere Religiously."

these ideas are not natural. They are the result of discourse created to serve the interests of institutions and their desire to remain unmoved.[107]

The narrative of loss associated with those learning to leave conventional religious participation is an example of how bodies and lives are governed and punished. Religious authorities deploy countermeasures that often cast individualism as a threat to conventional religious identity and commitment.[108] Deconstructing such power-filled governing efforts operating in contemporary theology would go far to fulfill the liberational goal at the core of our practice. As Terry Tempest Williams notes, "a closed system will not develop, nor will its members. Life requires difference to survive, and to thrive."[109]

Pastoral theologian Emma Percy suggests that despite the existing conventions, biases, and the ever-present asymmetry in power, vital and effective religious education and ministry endeavors to be an intersubjective "action" to develop virtues—not "work" to enforce rules.[110] She suggests that the action of encouraging and training people's ability to choose in contingent situations is the secret of maturity and a good life toward which all ministry should teach and preach today.[111] By contrast, the theology of affiliation implies that those who live in contingent religious spaces are deficient, so can be ostracized and treated as objects. I suggest instead that contemporary patterns of religious life and learning may have something constructive—not just alarming—to teach the larger church.[112]

A NEW PROPOSAL

Bringing disaffiliating religious persons into this dialogue begins with close studies of actual persons and practices in a liquid modernity characterized by movement and remixing. So how do we chart something in flux?

This book's title, *Out on Waters*, represents not only a generative metaphor of the phenomenon in question, but also suggests practical steps to be where the activity is. Just as nautical charts are constantly revised to reflect the changing realities of a body of water, so too teachers and leaders

---

107. Beaudoin, *Witness to Dispossession*, 3.
108. Beaudoin, *Witness to Dispossession*, 81.
109. Williams, *Refuge*.
110. Percy, *Mothering as a Metaphor for Ministry*, 85.
111. Percy, *Mothering as a Metaphor for Ministry*, 105.
112. Beaudoin, *Witness to Dispossession*, 85.

CONVERSION

Christian theologians and educators have long used the language of "conversion" to describe individual and collective experiences and movement associated with religious life and learning. In common usage, to "convert" has become synonymous with personal change. Religious conversion most often refers to a profound change in belief and practice pertaining to one's ultimate concern.[113] The multiple perspectives on conversion in Christian life and learning suggest both the complexity and significance of the experience the term is attempting to signify. Each contribution, in its own way, hints at significant dimensions to the experience and its importance in tradition: Conversion is the search for an adequate system of beliefs and practices in the ongoing process of becoming ourselves. Conversion is also the ongoing means by which tradition does more than preserve the past.

Yet in her essay "Conversion as Foundational to Religious Education," Mary Boys notes that in conventional discourse, the "one who leaves Catholicism to embrace another faith tradition is an 'apostate' not a convert. Someone who leaves the church has 'fallen away.'"[114] Although an individual has decided to take an alternative path of ongoing conversion, that choice and movement is not described as such. Such limits show the need for a new lens or language with which to chart new searches for adequate systems of values and beliefs. Without "turning conversion around,"[115] religiously significant movements that involve an exit from known categories of religiousness will be ignored or given punitive labels.

For this reason, Henri Gooren's work represents an important addition to the conversion discourse. Gooren opens up the conversation to accommodate mobility, choices, and change that happen over time, and that can include the remixing and disaffiliation we have surveyed. Although Gooren's use of the secular term "careers" to describe the process of ongoing conversions might seem strange, it illuminates the intersectional dynamics of conversion. In a religious field characterized by options, mobility, and remixing, religious affiliation is not unlike career choices. Religious

---

113. Boys, "Conversion as a Foundation of Religious Education."
114. Boys, "Conversion as a Foundation of Religious Education."
115. Boys, "Conversion as a Foundation of Religious Education."

choices before the present career are part of the process of ongoing learning and growth. The choice to disaffiliate is not a break from the past but an alternative direction taken for any number of reasons that also involves transferring what one has learned.

Gooren's "conversion careers" also include movements that often occur within an affiliated community and not simply between different groups.[116] These movements change levels of participation and involve development of more authentic expressions of religious identity.[117] Gooren's theory proposes an analytical model that distinguishes and explains various stages, not necessarily linear in progression, of religious participation where conversions and de-conversions are fluid and ongoing.[118] They are so because the tensions that conventional religious systems impose can lead religious learners to depart to search for more adequate religious beliefs and practices.

By pairing Gooren's contribution to conversion literature with religious educational perspectives, deconversion emerges as a significant element of religious life and learning worthy of study in its own right. Even when conversion is understood broadly as ongoing development, it can become meaningless if one does not recognize that there is no conversion without deconversion from previous beliefs, practices, and communities.[119]

DECONVERSION

Rather than implying deficiency, the language of deconversion suggests there is more at work in disaffiliation than an individualistic break in loyalty. Deconversion implies the religious significance associated with a profound and ongoing change in practice and belief in relation to what a person perceives as ultimate reality.[120] This experience begins when a religious learner, for the sake of spiritual fulfillment, authenticity, or a renewed sense of Divine presence deconstructs, in both personal and communal

---

116. Gooren, *Religious Conversion and Disaffiliation*, 48–49.

117. C. Bauman, "Conversion Careers."

118. See Gooren, *Religious Conversion and Disaffiliation*, 48–49; C. Bauman, "Conversion Careers."

119. Barbour, *Versions of Deconversion*, 3.

120. This represents a common meaning of conversion across disciplines. See James, *Varieties of Religious Experience*; Conn, *Conversion*; Loder, *Transforming Moment*; Moran, *Religious Education Development*; Peace, *Conversion in the New Testament*.

life, what has been provided and decides to search for more salient notions than what ecclesial authorities emphasize.[121] Allow me to address the term's possible negative connotations.

The English prefix *de-* comes from a Latin preposition indicating a movement "from, away from, out of." Many uses of the prefix suggest a loss of some sort—for example, the removal of something as in "deforest" or "dethrone." The prefix can also indicate the reversal of direction, as in "decompose." Although these uses imply a negative meaning, the prefix *de-* can also suggest a removal, cutting off, or closing off that is positive. Movement away from and leaving behind some options or removing obstacles to settle a dilemma and move forward, as is communicated in the English words "decide" or "determine," suggest positive movement and meaning. Moreover, the prefix *de-* can indicate a morally positive process and move away from something experienced as ethically problematic toward a new good, as in "desegregate."

Mary C. Boys provides a compelling example of this movement in her book *Has God Only One Blessing?* in which she shares the story of the Sisters of Our Lady of Sion, founded in 1840s France for the explicit purpose of converting Jews to Catholicism. The Sion Sisters as an order were decidedly supersessionist.[122] Yet individually and collectively the Sisters deconstructed their religious reality, determined that their Christian vocation (or career) was problematic, and decided to change it after an encounter with religious difference.

The Sisters discerned that the church's teaching concerning the Jewish community was flawed, and even contemptuous. They chose to take action that fundamentally altered how they viewed themselves and their mission. They learned this critical theological reflection by encountering the good and holy outside the boundaries they were provided.

Many factors contributed to this rejection of the church's *Adversus Judaeos* teaching, including many individual experiences of European Sisters witnessing the Shoah and hiding Jewish families from the Nazis. One

---

121. Nagle, "How We Get Somewhere Religiously."

122. While the jolting sentiments of this modern Christian history are difficult to hear, I think it significant to remember that it was in 1959 that Pope John XXIII removed this prayer from the source and summit of Catholic life, the Eucharistic liturgy:

"Let us pray for the unfaithful Jews, that our God and Lord may remove the veil from their hearts; that they also may acknowledge our Lord Jesus Christ . . . who drivest not even the faithless Jew away from thy mercy, hear our prayers, which we offer for the blindness of that people."

Sister explained the movement away from a "conversionist stance, with clear boundaries and certitudes to a dialogical way of life where boundaries are far less distinct." This Sister added that "this dialogical way of life requires us to live side by side with people different than ourselves."[123] In 1950, the community's leadership issued a letter critical of the church's teaching and their mandate. The letter recommended that members study Judaism and that they reverse their community's mission. Rather than working to convert Jews, the Sisters of Our Lady of Sion would now work to counter anti-Semitism.[124]

This decision caused consternation among the order's clerical supervisors and shook up the order itself. Although some Sisters remained in the order to live out their new mission, some left the community disillusioned. Others may have left Catholicism or occupied the margins of its reach. Boys argues that the church has much to learn from the Sion Sisters.

From the mendicants and the Reformation to liberation theology and the 12-Step Movement, the Christian tradition develops as its members respond to the world in which they live and to the G*d of their understanding. Individuals and communities exclude some elements, recall others, and reinvent the tradition as they contend with new questions.[125] Persons and groups drive this process by choosing what is essential and nonessential in religious life and learning. Like the Sion Sisters, these choices often contradict authoritative teaching. Religious education operates at this intersection of preservation and revelation, and drives this responsive process. Is our existing discourse adequate to include deconversion in the process of religious life and learning?

The deconversion and conversion of the Sion Sisters exhibits the aforementioned elements of: encounter with difference, choice, mobility, and remixing regardless of institutional boundaries established by external authority. They did in fact help alter the very sense of tradition we have inherited. And we are grateful for it. In that respect, their choices and action do represent a conversion. But not recognizing the distinct process of deconversion involved with departing from convention ignores a significant element in both individual and collective religious life and learning.

Through the lens of deconversion, the authenticity that drives much of contemporary religious life and learning, and even disaffiliation, can

---

123. Boys, *Has God Only One Blessing?*, 18.
124. Boys, *Has God Only One Blessing?*, 18.
125. Irwin, *Christian Histories, Christian Traditioning*, 41.

include a religious desire that brings what individuals and groups deem are the essential elements of tradition to new relational commitments and communities that feel more authentic and true. Deconversion literature offers a way to describe these movements between levels of participation that renegotiate expectations of adherence and affiliation that can lead to complete disaffiliation, or not.[126] Conversion and deconversion language helps us to appreciate the dynamic elements of a living tradition, including rejection, and the corresponding remix style of both Nones and Somes occurring in contemporary North America. I wonder: Might there be something good happening here?

---

126. Deconversion literature originated in a European context but has since become a shared term used by scholars to name the dynamics of deciding and determining to move away from conventional religious affiliation and turning toward another course of ongoing religious development.

Portraits from the Edge of Affiliation

chapter 2

THE THINKER AND THE GUIDE

The stories gathered and portrayed in this and the following chapters resonate with the research regarding a significant and growing portion of the population in the United States whose experiences, beliefs, and practices were learned from traditional religions that they are now challenging, along with the affiliation-based participation associated with them. This trend is especially pronounced in Roman Catholicism. Theological and religious educational discourse is working to catch up and develop adequate language to describe this phenomenon. The disaffiliating Catholic participants in this study also struggled for language to describe the space they occupy, the way they practice, and how they arrived there. They experience and express "religion" or "religiousness" as more dynamic and fluid than earlier generations have. Their portraits also suggest that persons who dwell in and pass through this space appear to move around institutional authority the way water flows around a rock.

PORTRAITURE: A UNIQUE VIEW

The researcher who asks first "What is good here?" is likely to experience a very different reality than one "who is on a mission to discover the source of failure."[1] Because of this insight, portraiture provides an intentionally generous and eclectic process to begin the conversation about deconversion and people who experience it. The methodology searches for what is good, but also assumes that the goodness found will include inconsistencies and imperfections.

---

1. Lawrence-Lightfoot and Davis, *Art and Science of Portraiture*, 9.

The Process behind This Portraiture

After initial conversations with sixteen religious educators in the New York City area, I invited four educators to participate in the study. During the preliminary interviews, I asked educators to identify a former student with whom they had a positive teaching experience but who nonetheless had departed from affiliated membership with the Catholic Church. Two of these educators decided they would not be able to identify and contact a former student due to the sensitivity of recent scandals and scrutiny in their schools. I have included them as a third portrait in chapter 3 because our conversations offer distinct insight regarding how the process of deconversion is affecting the teaching and learning of religion.

I initiated contact with the teacher-learner pair presented in portrait #1 by first meeting with the religious educator who then identified the former student. The second teacher-learner pair joined the study in the opposite order. The presentation of the individual subjects in their portrait pairs follows the order in which I encountered them.

Over the course of four months, I conducted in-depth, open-ended, semi-structured interviews, participant observations in the various educational settings, informal interviews with family members and colleagues, email conversations, and a final group interview to incorporate the experience of both learner and educator into the final portrait. The interview series with both the educators and former students followed a basic outline. The first interview concentrated on the details of their present experience: What it is like teaching religion? What is your religious life like now? The second interview focused on life history up to the present time: How did you become a teacher of religion? What were your most formative religious experiences? When did you first begin imagining alternatives to religious affiliation? The third interview was a group conversation exploring the meaning participants made of their teaching-learning relationship. This conversation also included reflection on the phenomenon of religious disaffiliation as a whole from their personal views.

In these conversations, I shared elements of my own story and experiences teaching where there was resonance. I situated myself alongside both the teachers and the learners, making the conversations more collaborative than interviewer driven. Although I came to each interview meeting with a basic question to structure our time together, I did not know what I was looking for until it emerged. However, certain primary questions did drive the study: How do religious educators and students in an educational relationship characterize the experience and result of religious learning when disaffiliation has been the result? Could disaffiliation be one possible outcome of a successful religious education? If so, how?

In order to generate useful knowledge in response to these questions, I listened for the voices, authority, and wisdom of the research participants themselves. The final product is a textured portrayal of the complexity of perspectives and experiences of persons negotiating the disaffiliation process and teaching in liquid modernity that I hope provokes you, the reader, to think more deeply about the multiple issues layered into the phenomenon of religious disaffiliation.

A LITTLE ABOUT THE PORTRAITIST

The interpretative nature of portraiture requires the artist's (or in this case, the writer's) rigorous reflexivity up front and throughout. My own positioning and perspective provide a significant lens through which the data was collected, analyzed, and interpreted.

As a theorist, I am out on the same waters as those with whom, and of whom, I am theologizing. This research, therefore, is biased—or, as Elizabeth Conde-Frazier says, it is "attached."[2]

I locate myself on the outskirts of Catholicism where I enjoy mutually critical and enhancing relationships with both religiously affiliated and disaffiliating individuals and communities. I am in many ways a "None," a "Some," and/or a "Deconvert." Like the participants in this study, I also feel at a loss for language that does not reduce my experience and development to a "lapsed," "former" or "individualistic rejection" of Catholic tradition. I was speaking truthfully in the preface when I said my religious formation was successful. Furthermore, because my hunch is that religious disaffiliation may represent something more than a failure of religious education and evangelization, seductive secular culture, or young adult narcissism, I feel accountable to both religious and "non"-religious communities and therefore seek to contribute to an interreligious educational and theological discourse that can operate with more than a narrative of loss or deficiency when speaking of and with those outside the boundaries of normative religious identity.

I am implicated, then, in this work as a both a teacher and a learner. I have experienced both sides of affiliation and now reside somewhere in

---

2. Conde-Frazier, "Participatory Action Research," 236.

between. Having done so has allowed me to teach effectively to a diverse group of students. The restoration of persons as primary theologians, regardless of their religious affiliation, represents a point of departure in my work. My professional commitment to ecumenical and interreligious relationships, including "Nones," "Somes" or "Deconverts" stems from the view that *they* are *us*.

The portraits follow a basic structure that allow the reader to experience the unique subject. There is an initial sketch of the pair, a description of meeting each individual, and thematic sections based on refrains that emerged during our conversations. Each portrait concludes by portraying the pairs in conversation, literally, during the group interview. The final product presented does not claim to be exhaustive nor does it reduce the complexity of the particular person or persons. It does, however, intend to make the complexity of disaffiliation more comprehensible.[3] While analysis is certainly occurring in and through the following portraits, a more structured analysis follows in chapters five and six.

PORTRAIT #1: THE THINKER AND THE GUIDE

An Initial Sketch

When I met with Michael, thirty-two years old, and Eliot, fifty-six years old, I had already spoken with them individually on a number of occasions. I was eager to sit down with them for our final interview because both men place a high value on reflection in their lives and each commented independently that our interviews had been a rare and welcome experience to talk about these questions. They also looked forward to speaking with one another. However, I was curious how the pair would discuss the potentially uncomfortable topic of religious disaffiliation that had developed since their time together as teacher and student.

Eliot grew up in what he described as a typical Catholic family of his generation. His parents participated in Catholic bowling leagues, the Holy Name Society, and the Women's Auxiliary. He admitted he has always felt a natural affinity for the Church. "I felt at home whether that was in the physical space or in the sacraments. . . . For whatever reason, I have always found the Mass powerful . . . well, not always," he admitted. "Sometimes I am bored out of my gourd, but what that gathering is saying, what it's

---

3. Lawrence-Lightfoot and Davis, *Art and Science of Portraiture*, 215.

connecting us to, still blows my mind every time I am there." Eliot never experienced what he called the "temporary disaffiliation" so common among young adults. An alumnus himself of an all-boys Catholic high school in the area, Eliot also earned advanced degrees in theology and explored a vocation as a Catholic priest. He feels that he was guided to a more authentic expression of his vocation to work within the Catholic tradition as a married man and religious educator.

Michael also spoke positively of his childhood in a Catholic household. There was no bowling league, but "Catholicity" was an early way he contextualized himself and others. Michael works in a consulting firm in Manhattan, and lives with his fiancée in Brooklyn. He is well traveled, and does not attend Mass regularly. While the ritual traditions of Catholicism still appeal to Michael, he and his fiancée are not planning a Catholic ceremony. His fiancée was raised Methodist and has a similar disaffiliated religious identity and worldview. Despite what others might determine as disaffiliated behavior, Michael does not believe he has "left" the Catholic tradition, or his relationship with G*d that was built in and through that tradition. He identifies proudly as a Catholic person but qualifies this identity. "I am Catholic sociologically." Michael concedes he does not have "a good label" for who he is religiously or spiritually.

Knowing these details of their religious lives, the two men appear an unlikely pair—even more so when sitting by side. Over six feet tall with a voice that carries like a baritone singer, Eliot commands attention. Michael is shorter and more softly spoken. However, his thoughtfulness holds space as much or more than Eliot's larger frame and volume. The superficial differences, including their difference in religious affiliation, obscure the more intangible elements that make up these two men. What these two share in common quickly became apparent and brought into focus what I had learned about Eliot as an educator and Michael as a learner: they both like to talk about things that matter. As we sat down together, there was an immediate and easy intergenerational banter between like-minded men.

Meeting Eliot

Eliot was charming throughout our conversations beginning with our very first phone call when he engaged me inquisitively concerning the theoretical foundations for the study. To say that Eliot is a charismatic teacher feels insufficient to portray the man and educator. He possesses a disarming swagger that can only be characterized as that of a man with a secret he is completely willing to share.

In our first interview, Eliot quoted a mentor as saying, "'If you want someone to give up their life for this thing you call your religion, I better see a hell of a lot of joy in your face, not the sourpuss.' . . . Joy may be too strong a word on most days, but I try to live that. It provides me meaning." Eliot presents Catholic tradition in a persuasive way that only authenticity can produce. Consciously or not, students in his class likely develop, at the very least, a belief that everything he says could very well be true. As Eliot himself puts it, "I have found something that quells the restlessness, not completely, but enough." Eliot is "evangelical" in the best sense of that term. He makes good known.

The principal of the Catholic prep school where Eliot teaches described him as an excellent, experienced, responsive religious educator. Eliot has taught religious studies and directed the Christian service program for just shy of thirty years. His principal explained that Eliot has a "Catholic way" of presenting material. "It is just who he is." He described the way Eliot effortlessly brings tradition to life by connecting tradition with contemporary experiences, and giving students the space to be where they are.

The clarity with which he responded during our first conversations at the New York Public Library about his hopes for his students, the realities of teaching religion today, and his own formative experiences that contributed to his theology and practice struck me. The detailed stories Eliot shared of his faith development and my observations of his teaching provide insight into the connection between the religious person and the religious educator. Eliot has never felt a tension between these identities. Like he did as a child, Eliot continues to feel at home in the Church. He attends Mass regularly and helps lead the RCIA team at his parish. His life is the source and vehicle for what he teaches. He shared with me, and with his students, that he teaches "this stuff" because it has worked for him. Eliot's teaching begins with experience, fosters open dialogue, and guides learners toward finding G*d in all things.

"The Church as It Is": A Critical Appraisal of the Institution

My observations of Eliot in educational exchanges and relationships exemplified his willingness to pose and entertain difficult questions that do not have easy or conventional answers. For example, he took two class periods to allow adolescent boys to debate the morality of premarital sex. He engaged their arguments without referencing scripture or the Catechism as the authority, but guided the boys to a similar morality discerned from their own previous experiences. At the end of these two class periods and their discussions, one outspoken student for promiscuity concluded respectfully, "I need to think more about this." In exchanges like these, Eliot does not shy away from sharing the reality that he himself wrestles with his faith and the tradition's relationship to his life. Religious life and religious tradition are complex and imperfect. Eliot's teaching shows that he accepts this complexity. In our conversations, he shared with me some core experiences that influenced his development and strong connection to the Church, including lessons concerning the Church's flaws. Eliot represents a significant case, as he is clearly an educator who guides some students to a deepened and affiliated relationship with the Catholic community (and some to decide to take alternative paths).

Eliot's earliest memory of religion was at the age of eight when he and his mother learned that he would not be allowed to serve as an altar boy because he was not a student in a Catholic school. His mother would not be deterred.

The priests involved with the training of altar boys made it as difficult as possible for Eliot to participate. His mother kept pushing—even learning Latin herself in order to teach him the Missal. Although she went toe-to-toe with Church leaders, she never suggested leaving the church. Eliot was the first public school altar boy in his parish, an experience he found wonderful. The experience taught Eliot three things: (1) how much his mother valued participation in the Church; (2) that the Church is imperfect; and (3) that the Church's limitations and errors are not deal breakers. This maturity concerning the mixed qualities of the Church continued to be a theme in Eliot's early life, and continues to influence his teaching style.

Eliot thrived in his theology classes at the traditional all-boys Catholic high school to which he transferred. He encountered progressive content and outstanding teachers. Eliot expressed gratitude and admiration for his religion teachers' openness to questioning. Eliot recalled how they would take students' questions and "just run with it." How these Brothers treated him as a student, not just what they taught him, made them some of his most significant teachers and models of religious education. However, a number of those Brothers, including the principal and vice principal, left the school and their order during Eliot's first year in high school.

> Not only did they leave, they left and married their secretaries! The Brothers who stayed had a hard time processing it. We all did. . . . It taught me again that the church is not a monolithic, consistent community that can live by rules alone. It was absolute chaos . . . yet, somehow there was an important thread that continued.

Eliot added that he has met some of those Brothers over the years in their new lives. "They are wonderful! It's okay that they left. . . . They're not traitors." He explained that he recognized the school for what it was during that time—like the church, not eternal and unchanging, but human and limited. "But even flawed human beings can surprise you and do something where you realize you may just be witnessing the Spirit at work." Eliot suggested that this humility is part of growing up religiously.

"When in Doubt, I Lean toward Being Open, Absolutely": A Practical Theology

Eliot never planned to become a teacher. After finishing his undergraduate degree and earning an MA in ethics, he went to work researching and reporting on medical ethics. His path to religious education and formation began when he met two teachers visiting the center where he worked. The more Eliot heard about teaching religion in high school, the more he felt it was something he wanted to do. When a job opened up, he took it and has not looked back. Eliot shared that he cannot imagine a job better suited to him. "I feel like God set me in the right direction." Eliot's teaching style, even his classroom, demonstrates an ongoing dialogue between the affinity for the church that began in his childhood, and his openness to other sources of revelation.

His classroom seems equal parts chapel and man cave. The room is small for the twenty-five to thirty boys sitting in it. There is little empty space on the walls. They are covered with Da Vinci sketches, religious icons, photographs of cathedrals, along with framed posters of Jerry Garcia, The Beatles, and significant sport pages from the Mets' history. A large banner centrally located on the far wall dominates and organizes the assemblage. What even the attention-deficient student in his classes walks away with, at the very least, is: Religion = Finding God In All (*these*) Things.

Talking about his hopes for his students and his goals as an educator, Eliot shared,

> My hopes for my students during and after my classes are that they see that religion is relevant to their lives and to the questions that every life ought to engender, and that despite some of the mistakes the Church has made historically, there's still a treasure chest of wisdom that I think includes the best of the human tradition, philosophy and the arts and the like, but there's also this additional element that I believe only comes from revelation. That God or the power, the force, whatever, that is responsible for all of existence seeks this personal relationship with you, that loves you to the point where it would come into creation as a person without any privilege and accompany us and teach us and die for us. That, as Tertullian said, is certain because it's impossible. No human could make up that story and expect anybody to buy it.

In order to reframe religious questions for an audience that thinks they have heard it all before, Eliot takes his students to the boiler room the first day of class. In the dark and unfamiliar room, he has them imagine they are being brought into existence and this is their reality. "What questions do you want to ask?" When his students suggest "Where are we? What is this stuff around us? What are we supposed to do here?" Eliot then responds:

> These are the great questions for any human being to address at the core of his or her being, and at the core of religion. Religion is one of the ways humanity has set out to respond to the questions that life ought to engender with doctrine, ritual, and symbol. Let's go back to the classroom and with that in mind I want you to spend the year thinking about how adequate the responses we're going to study are. I want you to always feel free to raise your hand and say this either doesn't make sense or I think you're trying to ram some BS down our throats.

The reason for this approach, Eliot explained, was that if religious education is not a conversation in which he is meeting his students where they are, "then it's a colossal waste of time for both of us." Though there are long stretches when he and his students just have to get through curriculum and tests and GPA, Michael confirmed these elements of the unexpected in Eliot's classes that instilled awe and wonder.

In addition to his surprising classroom style, Eliot shared another detail of his personal life that was a little unexpected. Like many of their generation, his own young adult children no longer attend church and have an ambiguous relationship with the institutional elements Catholicism. So

I asked, "If your kids are disaffiliating, what do you think that means?" He responded with a clarity that indicated this was not the first time he had wrestled with the question.

> I don't know if it's rationalization, but this is between them, G*d, and the Holy Spirit. I've just got to be a role model. . . . I've been humbled by how little I have known that's turned out to be true in my life, and even more humbled by what I thought was absolutely true in my life and has turned out not to be. That openness, I think . . . comes from when I see Jesus in the scriptures, and experience Him in the Mass. That is the God I resonate with. That it is ok. He says, "I want you to work your ass off, and I want you to be humble, but I want you to have a sense of humor, and I want you to care about every single person that's in need because everyone is an instance of my son or my daughter." Some days that's easier than others . . . but when in doubt, I lean towards being open. Absolutely.

"Being Right vs. Being Good": A Formative Experience

Eliot learned this humility and openness both in and out of the classroom. He has never experienced a division between his identity as a religious person and as a religious educator. Eliot's own ongoing religious life and learning shapes his theology and teaching practice. His two most influential professors in college were not Catholic, yet they imparted the importance of humility. "That's part of what the faith journey is. You do your best to understand and embrace the truth but you realize there's been hell of a lot of people, a hell of a lot smarter than me who got it wrong." Eliot shared that they taught him humility in terms of holding others to account for what he believes. "I don't think in those terms anymore."

In graduate school, Eliot focused on academics more than spirituality or ministry, but attended Mass faithfully. There was a great parish near campus that kept him connected. He admitted comfortably that he was not really dating much, not for lack of trying. So, having always felt close to the church, he did what young single Catholic men do: he thought about becoming a priest. Then he met the woman who would become his wife. They dated for nine years before they got married. "I loved the church and what it represented, and its message, but living as a priest was not going to make me fully alive." He referred to being married as one of his most formative experiences. "I don't think I would have developed as a person without having somebody to share that journey with... somebody to tell you, 'You're being an ass. Stop it.'" All these experiences built upon what Eliot explained was the most formative lesson of his life: the lesson he learned from his family.

Eliot shared that around the age of eight, he began to notice that his father came home "a little out of focus."

> I can still hear it, the pop of a Schmidt's beer bottle. Whether it was eleven a.m. or twelve a.m., that just marked that it was going to be a different day. So I would make myself scarce.... He never laid a hand on us, never got fired, but just that change, it was not desirable for anybody.

Eliot has given retreat talks about his experience as the child of an alcoholic and shares it in his classes when teaching the Paschal Mystery. Eliot often framed the value he places on religious life and learning in terms of getting through the "crap storms that are sure to come, if they haven't already, and will come again and again." He explained in one interview, "I tell my students: you will suffer like everyone else. You may even suffer for taking a stand for justice . . . but do you believe that through Good Friday there is an Easter Sunday coming after? If the answer is yes, and there is a community to share that grief with in dialogue with tradition, you can receive graces that you otherwise would not receive through suffering." A prominent characteristic of Eliot's religious biography centers on making sense of suffering. The seeds of this faith were planted and tested early on.

Eliot's parents grew apart due to the pain his father caused, and they finally separated. Despite his father's addiction, Eliot spoke honestly about the religious lessons he learned from his dad:

> He was a very democratic man in terms of how he related to people. There was nobody he didn't pay attention to and have a good laugh with. He knew the restaurant owner's name, the waiters, and the busboys. They'd joke around together. In retrospect, I see that as a very, very important religious disposition that had nothing to do with religion explicitly, but to me it was as important as anything I've ever learned.

Eliot then spoke of the most significant lesson that accompanied this suffering, a lesson taught him by his mother.

Eliot's father worked as a custodian in a nearby town and died at fifty-three years old. His father was also smoker. Eliot recalled noticing a lump on the side of his father's neck when he was visiting him at his apartment.

"It just grew and grew. Long story short, oncologist, lymphoma, radiation, and then they finally called us in and said, 'There is nothing we can do. So it's time to prepare.'" This is how they prepared:

> One day my mother called my brother and sister and me into the living room and said, "We're going to bring your dad home." We set up a hospital bed in my bedroom on the first floor. I slept on the couch and took care of him for probably two months. . . . He was sober the whole time. . . . My father taught me to play baseball and golf. He set up a little dark room in our basement for black and white pictures. . . . I have a lot of great memories but it just turned south. . . . To have those two months where he was at his best, and always had his sense of humor. . . . It was the best two months that I can remember in terms of relating to him. . . .
>
> My mom bringing my dad home as he was dying is probably the most important lesson I have ever learned. For my mom to be able to want to do that, to bring him home, that is the most formative experience of my life. . . . She taught me an important distinction, one that I wish more people understood: There is a difference between being right and being good. It's important to do the right thing, and to know what the right thing to do is, but there's sometimes a higher calling in a situation.

Eliot spoke earnestly of feeling G*d's presence during this time, even recalling his father's humorous spirit manifesting itself among his family when that spirit had left his body. The morning his father died, Eliot dreamt of running toward the empty tomb under a warm sun. He felt serenity and peace. When Eliot woke up, he did not hear the accustomed labored breathing in the next room. He awakened his mother, brother, and sister. "We all stood around his bed, held hands, said a prayer, and talked about how much we loved him. Then my brother said, 'Geez. I hope he's dead because otherwise he is going to be very alarmed by all this.'" Eliot laughed out loud telling this part of the story and explained, "That would've have been my father's line."

Eliot teaches and converses with this level of both gravitas and humor. He embodies the teaching that hangs centrally located in his classroom, of "Finding G*d in All Things." The discernment of G*d in his experiences and emotions has changed both his life and his approach to teaching his students.

One of the reasons Eliot hoped Michael would choose to participate in the study was because Michael was one of the few students in his long career that had really absorbed more than the "corny stuff" he does in the classroom. Eliot recalled, "Michael wrestled with ideas not be because they were going to be on the next test. You could tell he just wanted to mull them over."

MEETING MICHAEL

Even after hearing the Eliot's memories of him, I must admit I had some preconceived notions of what a graduate of an elite East Coast prep school would be like. Michael quickly dismantled my pre-judgments. Scheduling a convenient time and place to meet took a little time, but Michael was responsive and active in making time despite what was clearly a busy period between work and wedding planning.

We met in the middle of the business day in midtown Manhattan. Michael arrived early and politely would not let me buy him a cup of coffee. And before I realized it, he had paid for my bottle of water.

Michael looks a young thirty-two years old. He wears glasses and his hair cropped short, along with a suit and tie. What struck me meeting Michael was a dissonance between the business dress and the man with whom I was speaking. I also work in midtown Manhattan. In that context, one is not accustomed to the thoughtful speech and patience with which Michael communicates. Our conversation was intense and interesting almost immediately, and was anchored by Michael's thoughtful responses. He works in a high stress job; I imagined his patience and reflective disposition translating effectively into corporate meeting rooms. We both literally leaned into an engaging exchange of questions and comments concerning his and others' religious lives and learning.

When I asked Michael about his upcoming wedding, I was curious whether he and his fiancée's choice to live together and not have a Catholic wedding was hard for his friends and family. Michael explained that he had not felt any judgment from his family, but that his fiancée's parents were a little concerned about them living together, but for gendered rather than religious reasons. Michael did add, however, that he thought Eliot might have an opinion about it—Eliot had in fact mentioned it with a little concern—but added, "It's not something I feel guilty about . . . I thought about it, I made a decision, and I am ok with it." As for their wedding, Michael shared:

> The religiosity of the event does not come from being in a church necessarily or needs to be provided by a priest. I think it's about

the event itself.... I think that suffices.... Instead of the religious quality being given to the event externally, it is coming from a more internal expression of us. If that can come from inside yourself, that is better—in my opinion—than just sitting in front of a priest in a church.... I think it makes sense to do that if you have a relationship with a church and a priest.... In this new era of thinking, I am not going to get married by someone I don't have a relationship with. We are both not churchgoers, so the option is to find a priest that we're comfortable with, go to some services, and maybe never go again. Or have someone who knows us well and a have a nice thoughtful ceremony that means something to us. That seems more appropriate, but you are going against tradition.

Despite how it might sound, tradition matters to Michael.

"Proudly Catholic": A Disaffiliating Identity?

Michael is not sure he has left the Catholic tradition. He explained in our first interview that being Catholic has always been an identity for him. "If I say to someone I am Irish Catholic from where I grew up, they immediately know me and I know them in a social identity way that someone who is Baptist from South Carolina is not going to." Michael identified proudly as a Catholic but qualified this identity by adding that he was both "an Irish Catholic" and "Catholic sociologically," explaining that, to him, "religious" meant "going to church." Being "spiritually Catholic" included Catholic belief and theology. Identifying as "Catholic sociologically" meant the cultural context that shaped and continues to shape him. When I asked what was keeping a sociological Catholic from joining the community, Michael laughed insightfully at the irony and replied:

> Why don't I go to church? Well, I will say this. I wish I went to church more. I will start there. The reason that I don't is that as much as it's been a habit to go to church, it's become a habit to not go to church. But I do wish I went more frequently. I like the idea of it being a reset of your week. A time to reflect.... And as an Irish Catholic, there is some guilt that I don't go, but not enough to drive me to go to church....
>
> Although I don't go to church anymore, I love the Triduum. ... I really love Good Friday, Holy Thursday, the whole Triduum. To me, it's what all the rest of Catholic ritual is based upon. It is so beautiful together.... I love the ritual.... My educational background is the Classics. I find the historical progression of

the Pagan religions, into the early church, and Muslim influences fascinating. I feel the Catholic Mass captures a lot of the collision of those traditions. . . . When I go to Mass, that's what I think about. . . . I learned that in Eliot's class. . . . The Church was not stamped out as one thing and is not unchanging. . . . I guess I don't go anymore because I have lots of frustrations with the Church: Its resistance to move forward, all the obvious abuses over the past fifteen years, . . . I just got in the habit of living my life without the constant church presence.

Michael explained that while he loves the ritual and sacrament of Catholic liturgy, he often leaves Catholic Mass bothered by the message of the homily. He articulated frustration at taking the time to participate in the ritual "only to leave the gathering feeling very anti-church." He admitted it did not happen every time, but with enough frequency that it has changed his religious behavior. He repeated that while he has developed a new habit of not going to church, being Catholic is still a part of his identity and its practices provide meaning in his life now—but some have taken on new forms and expression.

Although he has "departed the obligation" of going to church, Michael explained he has not "departed [his] relationship with G*d." He discussed an expansive theology learned from exposure to diverse points of view, including those presented in his formal religious education. He became suspicious of exclusive teaching having witnessed different "social contracts" that religions and cultures use to maintain order and talk about the Divine. Michael explained that he does not believe these social constructs should be exclusive, but observed that is how they are often taught and received. He shared that being strictly Catholic or having a strictly Catholic view is just as narrow and dangerous as when Catholics accuse other religions of the same behavior. "My mindset is not exclusive," he asserted. "I don't feel like I have left anything because there's nothing to leave from. It [Catholicness] is a relationship with God. It is not 'we are in this box, and you're not.' We are all together and the boxes don't matter in the end."

"Which Side I Sit On": Religious Identity Development in the Presence of Others

As a child, Michael attended an ethnic Italian parish in a diverse neighborhood. "I knew I was Catholic because when we went to Mass, the Catholics sat on one side and the Italians sat on the other." He shared that although he did not yet understand the difference between Catholics and non-Catholics, he was aware difference existed beyond the Italians on the other side of the aisle. There was a synagogue a few blocks from his home; his uncle was Jewish; and one of his aunts and her family had converted to an Evangelical Christianity. "So I knew there were other religions, but I was a kid. We're all the same. Everyone is a kid. That is all that matters."

In high school, Michael began to learn what it meant to be Catholic or not. During this time, he identified as Catholic socially, religiously, and spiritually. I asked if he thought learning what it meant to be Catholic narrowed his notion of religiousness. He paused briefly and replied, "No," that it became more focused, but not narrow. While he learned what it meant to be Catholic, because his school was not very diverse he had not yet really experienced anything to compare with what he had been taught. But, according to Michael, his religious education opened him to what else was out there and prepared him for when he would encounter a non-Catholic world.

Michael participated in the Ignatian Exercises in his high school, played football, went on retreats, and helped lead service trips. Michael thought his education in general, and religious education in particular, trained him both to identify and transgress categories.

> I was learning physics from a priest. Calculus from a priest. Teachers who obviously focused their life on something that's not calculus but then is also teaching calculus because they are an expert in calculus, not because they're the only guy they could find. I was taught by people who had deep, interesting connections with, not just religion, but other subjects. And I never had a priest as a religious studies teacher.

From his initial awareness of other religions in his neighborhood and family, his religious educators revealed to him that other religions not only existed but also had always been mixing with each other throughout history. Eliot's class, Church History, revealed to Michael the rich and complex story of Western civilization. Michael suggested that this readied him to be open to the otherness he himself would rub up against. Michael, for example, mentioned realizing that while he was studying Hebrew Scriptures it was also stirring questions of modern day Judaism, as well as a desire to speak with and learn from people living that faith.

The Thinker and The Guide

Michael articulated that his classes in high school were a departure from the "being-taught-what-to-think" education of parochial school. While he cannot remember much of the content of individual religious studies classes he attended, he recalled what he learned. His first year he learned that Scripture was a collection of books that had been edited and translated. The stories contained in the Bible changed from historical truth to literature that had a purpose and needed to be interpreted. Sophomore year he reported again that he had "no idea what we talked about in class" but learned because his teacher "clearly struggled with the same things we were." Michael learned that everyone is going to struggle. "So get used to it." This level of honesty regarding the challenge of religious life and learning spoke to Michael. He explained that Eliot's class fell into this category as well.

> The class was taught by someone who was in the middle of this struggle trying to help us make sense of what appears to be a little bit of nonsense. What is written in these textbooks, what we're supposed to believe is a little nonsensical in a lot of ways. So how do you handle that? How have people for the past two thousand years handled that? It was a practical approach to history. What does it all mean? What do the sacraments mean in relation to life? What are they telling you? Why are they important?

Michael learned, as Eliot explained it, the questions "any life ought to engender."

Beyond those questions, Michael learned that his teacher was reflecting on his own experiences and sharing what he himself had experienced, who he had become, and why he thought it mattered.

> I had really great religious education from men that brought the best of themselves and were honest about what they were struggling with. . . . The honesty was disguised in the curriculum and it is why it was so effective. I feel like anyone could take a textbook and just go through it. You can read a textbook and learn what it says. But that's not what religious learning is about. It's about connecting with what is in tradition through those relationships.

The year Michael spent in Eliot's class was significant in light of this honest struggle, as well as the suffering so central to Eliot's teaching. It was 2001 in New York City. In addition to the collective trauma of September 11, two of Michael's classmates committed suicide that year. Eliot described those months after 9/11 as a series of challenging teaching moments where as a religious educator he hoped to "adjust [his students'] image of G*d in a way that would serve them well for the rest of their mature lives." For example, one of Michael's classmates might share about how lucky he was that G*d had acted so that his mom's car did not start that morning while a classmate's uncle three desks over had died. Eliot remembered asking his classes to think about, "What are you claiming about G*d, if G*d somehow flooded the engine of your mother's car but not somebody else's?" It was in discussions like these, and in that challenging year, that Michael was shown how to respond to and reflect on his life. His motivation, Eliot observed, was not academic but the desire for a personal encounter with the material being studied, and the reflective process being demonstrated. Michael confirmed that his religious education prepared him for the next steps in his adult religious life.

After graduation, Michael attended college in the South where he encountered students ranging from fundamentalist Evangelicals to extreme Atheists. Michael found contrast to the beliefs and identity he had learned in his family and schooling. He heard characterizations and experiences of Catholicism that he had never encountered before. However, this exposure was not shattering, but thought provoking.

> I wondered what being Catholic meant exactly? There is so much dogma in the Catholic tradition and so much precedent that if you were to be a strict catholic, your life would be pretty specific and constrained. The way we each have gotten around that is that we each kind of have our own belief system. Right? That's how it really plays out. . . . Strict adherence like they were describing Catholicism was not something I had ever thought about or experienced as being Catholic. . . . That wasn't the religious curriculum I learned in high school. My grade school was like that, but I didn't put much credence in that kind of conventional religion. . . . I learned a very broad thought process and a very deep philosophical tradition.

Like his experience in high school, his religious identity did not narrow with this educational encounter; it became more focused and reflective. But he admitted that it did begin to loosen his affiliation.

After graduation, Michael chose to live in the Holy Land because "he wanted to better understand the religious conflict." That was his reason. It was that simple. He surmised that was not going to happen through reading a book. Michael worked for a small Christian international development company and lived with a Palestinian family. He became close with this family and with his coworkers. The experience was transformative.

> Maybe it was a religious experience, but not in a religious way. . . . There were months of having nothing to do but think, write, and try to understand what was going on. There was a lot of time for reflection. . . . I don't know how to describe it, but it felt like being at the center of something. . . . A lot of my thinking on the social construction of religions started when I was in the Holy Land. You can't help but think that a lot of people thinking about the same thing in just slightly different ways have been killed over that difference. . . . I think I learned a lot about myself and my approach to things. When I was in the Holy Land, I feel like *I* defined who I was. What made *me* tick and who I was as an adult. I don't think I knew that at the time, but I left there with something fundamental. It was growing up, I guess. That was the internal take-away. Externally I learned you can't always take for granted how religious things are presented.

Persistent Tradition: The Religiousness That Remains

Part social commentary, part confession, Michael shared that one feature of the contemporary culture he notices is the expectation and ability to choose the very best of something. In what he described as "hipster culture," there is a desire to do something as well as one can. Whether it is craft beer or artisan shaving instruments, Michael observed its influence "on the mindset of a certain group of the population. Mainly elites, who can afford to think in those terms." They have a desire for innovation that creates a more preferred future. Michael compared this to the contemporary religious situation where other young people are not joining institutional religions. "You've been exposed to a broad range of ideas, philosophies, theologies religions, cultures, you can't help but select the things you like and not the things you don't." As Drescher argues, how could religion be anything but a choice in this context? Michael has mixed feelings about this practice but believes it fits contemporary experience.

Within this tension, Michael did express a personal need for quiet times to unwind and spend time with people he cares about. Tradition continues to open out in the reality of Michael's everyday life in these personal and relational ways. Michael prays. "My prayer is reflection and the repetition of prayers that I've been saying forever. I'll say a couple Hail Mary's and Our Fathers, that kind of stuff. My prayer is a discourse with G*d." He explained that while communal structured time for reflection might be missing in his life, it is not simply the fault of contemporary culture. Michael is not the kind of person who joins groups easily. He works in a small firm and there are many young people. Many of these coworkers go to bars, restaurants, and spend time together outside of work. "I've never been that kind of person. . . . I just don't have that personality and I'm not comfortable in that kind of setting," Michael lit up when he remembered there was one colleague with whom he does very much enjoy speaking.

He explained that he and this coworker connect because they are not happy at work. The job is something at which they are both good, but both find it too "transactional" and insufficiently "transformational." When I asked him what they talk about, Michael warned that I was going laugh. (And I did, a little.) "We always talk about what we would do if we could do anything." His colleague dreams of becoming a child psychologist, or child social worker. As for Michael: "I'd love to make pizza."

> It's so methodical. . . . One thing I don't think society allows for, particularly in the digital age, is that no one is a master of anything anymore. Everyone is a generalist. . . . I think it would be interesting to be really focused on one thing if you enjoy it, and receive something from it. I think that is desirable. . . . Pizza for example, you're never going to make the same thing twice. You might do the same thing, with all the same ingredients but it's always a little different. That's a cool thing. To be able to follow the same physical process and yet you come out with something that's never the same as the one before. That is so appealing. The methodical piece, and the repetition. The let's do one thing different this time, or let's do it better this time, or let's change that. Whatever we do it's going to be a little different, so let's see what comes out. That speaks to me.

For similar reasons, Michael also loves to garden. He claimed a certain spiritual aspect to it and confessed it might speak to his introverted tendencies. That said, he explained he enjoys dealing with the "living, breathing world" and the humility and patience that comes from working with other organisms and putting one's hand in the earth.

Tradition does matter to Michael. The reflective affinity for ritual shows up in his life and in his young family. Though Michael and his fiancée do not attend church on Sundays, they have initiated a ritual meaningful to them both. When he and his partner are both home, they cook soup together.

It's not explicitly religiously or it's only obliquely religious. It's just this event to be together, the soup takes a while to make, and the smell of the soup rises up like an offering, like it says in Hebrew Scripture. I think it started because I was traveling for a whole year, so Monday morning I was out the door at six a.m. This was the only time during the week where, you know Saturday is always busy running around doing laundry, chores, and errands. So Sunday was it. So we decided to stop doing anything after a certain time and just hang out together. It also had a practical benefit. If we made enough soup, she would have enough for two or three more nights. So it became a thing we do. I think she would see it similarly. It is an important time for both of us, soup or no soup, just to spend Sunday night together unwinding. It's not a date night. Certainly not. There is no pressure to find a place to go. It is a let's have a glass of wine and just hang at home with no agenda. We fold laundry. I'll call my folks. She'll call hers.

You know Michael Pollan, the food journalist? In his most recent book, he talks about having a ritual where he is trying to perfect bread. I love the idea of making the bread and trying different things with his son, and having that time together. That's where I got the idea for Sunday night dinner. "What if we just did something the same every week? That sounded really nice. And it is. It has become a ritual. . . . That is probably why we do it. That's why church is church."

Sunday night dinner is a consistent embodiment of the complex but coherent religious life and learning Michael had shared with me. He and his fiancée do want to start a family and would like to pass on to their children this ritual element of his religious background. However, he expressed doubt that his habit of not going to church would change as they start a family.

I guess my feelings about going to church could change. I don't know how much it would. . . . There's the going to church, and there's this relationship. Going to church as a habit is not there anymore. But the relationship [with G*d] has remained. I would like to pass that on to our children. When I was growing up, my mother would pray with me at night. Then we'd just talk. Even as I got older, prayer at home always included this kind of open discussion with my parents. There is a comfort that comes from doing that together. That is one beautiful thing about church, I think. You share something, but you also think about it differently. That is the point of the conversation. And it is also the point that you are supposed to come to your own understanding. . . . I think that experience would be nice to share with children.

Michael admitted that planning the next phase of his life has reminded him of the reflection he learned to value in his religious education. He particularly identified the inclusion of nonreligious and non-Catholic concepts into this practice of discernment of G*d in all things. Michael explained proudly that his religious training formed him to be comfortable "going outside of religion to find religious answers . . . or going outside of being Catholic to find spiritual answers." He spoke more specifically by relating this preparation to his current religious identity. "I learned you might have to go somewhere else . . . you don't have to find all your peace, all your answers, in one place. My teachers never actually said that, but it is something I learned from them." I shared with Michael that his comments were striking because Eliot had said something very similar.

Michael: That's funny because we never talked about it like that. He probably never said it that way in class, ever, but I heard it. I guess that's the point [laughing]. That's very interesting.

Interviewer: Indeed, it is.

FINAL PORTRAIT: "PUT IT IN THE WIN COLUMN"

Before Eliot and Michael met with me to discuss the experience they shared from their different perspectives, Eliot gave me his impression of other alumni who come back in their twenties and thirties. Very few are still involved in the church, but he observed that his former students have not lost their orientation toward the good. "Many are great young men committed to service, and have re-appropriated what they do believe in and see as the best of the tradition they learned." Eliot's comments captured what I was finding by exploring other contemporary teacher-learner relationships. For that reason, Eliot particularly enjoyed the format of this study. He shared that he often wished he could meet with former students as part of a reunion weekend for a final course to listen to where they were and "hit them with a couple more lessons." Sitting in Bryant Park, Eliot had something like that opportunity with Michael and, serendipitously, it did occur on the school's reunion weekend.

As the three of us spoke, Eliot shared that as a high school student Michael recognized that what he was trying to do in class was present the topic of church history in a way that could be applied to one's life more broadly. He described the younger man across from him as a patient and disciplined student who absorbed perspectives, practices, thought, and ideas from any kind of tradition if he could see their value and relevance. "So, it was on me as an educator to communicate it in a compelling manner." If Eliot felt it was up to him to present and guide Michael through a broad and applicable meaning of church history in compelling manner, he did so. Michael's appreciation of living tradition and ritual is a testament to this. In many ways, however, it appears to have been a collaborative educational encounter.

Eliot shared with Michael that his typical evaluation of a student included initially discerning what it was that a particular learner needed him to be in order to grow: "Good cop, bad cop, does he need another parent, a scholarly-figure, a friend-figure?" Eliot shared that with Michael he felt he was able to, and ought to, relate to the young man as himself from the start. As an educator, I felt this was a significant revelation and an integral piece of a very different type of teaching. What occurs in such a teaching and learning relationship is an unpredictable and transformative process for both subjects, and the subject of study. In terms of teaching religion, what these two shared gives texture both to the confluence of cultural circumstances that makes the edge of affiliation a place—and to how deciding to pursue alternative paths of ongoing religious development may be a successful outcome of religious education.

Michael spoke of his teacher as a trusted guide through religious tradition because of his mastery of the content, but more so because he taught from the authority of his own struggles that he shared with his students. Michael felt that his guide was preparing him for a similar struggle of his own. Eliot realized Michael was going on the journey with or without him. As a teacher-guide, he shared what had worked for him.

Sarah Tauber, in *Open Minds, Devoted Hearts*, explains that the personal expression of a teacher-guide invites learners through explicit and implicit cues to pose challenging questions and propose new perspectives.[4] In his classes, Eliot often punctuated lectures or activities with explicit permission to "call BS" on certain ideas if his students were not buying it. He shared with me, "I have a job to teach what the Church teaches. That said, I want to hear their reaction to that. I believe my students feel they can say

---

4. Tauber, *Open Minds, Devoted Hearts*.

anything and ask anything in class and it's not going to trigger a violent response from me. That's the best part of the job, I could do something else if I weren't really interested in what they were thinking."

Michael shared that he learned most from Eliot when his teacher taught "religion with a light touch." Michael explained that his classes did not feel like religion classes—"like you were being told what to believe, what was right or wrong." Michael learned that being religious, or being Catholic, was something that developed. "I learned that religion changes and that my teachers wanted me to ask questions." Michael stated that he internalized that and that it has opened him up to new things. His religious education gave him "the framework to assess new experiences and [the] curiosity to seek them."

Michael described his experience in Eliot's class as a time when he was not "changing beliefs as much as learning, understanding, and building my own religious identity." Eliot nodded often during this conversation and added after this exchange that what Michael described "marks the difference between authentic religious education and education in some other Catholic schools where it is sort of pushing tradition into a student and expecting the students to act like sponges and absorb it." He explained that when he was teaching Michael and his classmates, he wanted to know what these young men experienced and what gave them a sense of awe and wonder, and where they had suffered. Eliot wanted to share how tradition might be able to speak to that.

Tauber points out that the effectiveness of this approach depends on educators asking the learners to share and reflect upon their experiences in a manner that encourages the learners to make their own decisions and informed choices.[5] In so doing, the teaching-learning relationship becomes one between a competent learner and a compelling guide that involves deconstruction and reconstruction of existing views for the sake of something new that can lead into a process of both conversion—and maybe deconversion. Eliot invites his learners into this type of reflective and interpretive process as he guides them through the difficult work of relating tradition to their lived experiences.

During and since Eliot's mentoring, Michael developed an enduring belief in G*d, openness to otherness, criticism of exclusive or oppressive rhetoric, and an ongoing faithful but critical praxis that organizes his life. Guides like Eliot showed him the passion, depth, and value of Catholic

---

5. Tauber, *Open Minds, Devoted Hearts*, 112.

tradition, but also exposed him to its flaws, and to other religious views. Those experiences in the classroom and beyond affected how he views himself religiously, spiritually, and socially. Learning from teachers who were honest about their own stances, struggles, and questions taught him that religion with less of an emphasis on exclusivism and empowered him to be able to "have conversations like this," he said with a smile—meaning the questions we were exploring together in this study.

> To be able to identify myself, who I am, and be confident in that. To understand what I believe, regardless of whether it is line with Church dogma. My religious education got me ready for the next steps of learning in my life. Regardless [of] where it took me, it got me ready for the context I live in and am comfortable with.

Michael was grateful for being prepared to deal with the challenging questions of life, and despite his ambiguous relationship with the institutional Church today, he characterizes his Catholic religious education as "successful and effective." He did note the dissonance this may cause for some: "I don't think that Church leaders would say the same thing, but I would say it was successful. Absolutely."

Eliot and I both exchanged glances during this conversation with Michael. Eliot realized the question would return to him. When I asked Eliot what he thought of what Michael was saying, he was reminded of Thomas Merton's well-known prayer from *Dialogues with Silence*: "Lead me by the right road, even if I know nothing about it." After listening to Michael, Eliot wondered aloud, "Maybe church isn't necessary right now. If you have found something that feeds you, go for it."

I had asked Eliot in an earlier conversation if it is important to him that his students affiliate religiously. He hesitated and noticed the tension that could surface, but admitted more quickly than I anticipated, "That's a good question. My gut says no, it's not." He went on to qualify that response:

> I believe that we're all on a quest to find that which will still the restlessness of our heart. I have found it for the most part—not completely—in the Catholic faith and being affiliated with the Church, but I recognize that most of the great saints have gone through times when they've struggled with the Church, or Church authority, or even Church teaching. So to wander away from it at some point for some length of time does not freak me out like I think it does some....

> I sometimes worry about the kids who are gung-ho affiliated, and what are the reasons why they are, and how does that translate into the way they live their life and the way they live their marriage and their parenting and their relationships with others who don't share that experience? I'd probably have much more in common and have a few more laughs and sweet moments with somebody who's disaffiliated but searching than I would with somebody who's affiliated for the wrong reasons.

Eliot and Michael agreed that the rise of disaffiliation is not surprising given the changes in culture, and further agreed that the Catholic Church has brought some of it on itself. Eliot added that he is not an alarmist and does not think there is a golden age to which to return. He explained that he has a real faith that in and through young people like Michael, and with the Holy Spirit, the Catholic Church might be "laboring into a new era of understanding, which may be more Christian when we come out on the other end, but that said, I'm still concerned. . . . I teach this stuff because it has worked for me. I worry my kid's generation won't have a tradition to lean on." His concern, faith, and humility exemplify the complex but coherent range of experiences and sources from which Eliot draws as he meets students where they are, fosters open and critical dialogue, and guides students to find G*d in all things.

Eliot is well trained theologically and the experiences of his childhood have formed him into a knowledgeable and humble religious guide for others who live, move, and make their meaning in a challenging world. The deeply embedded and central value of "finding G*d in all things" organizes and appreciates the complexity of religious life and learning. Being with his former student gave me a good sense of Eliot's commitment to and trust in the dignity of each individual learner, and ultimately to the revelation that may be occurring well outside his control.

Teachers like Eliot show learners like Michael new ways of exploring and developing their religious life. Their teaching guides students through the difficult and challenging elements, and even across some boundaries, by modeling honest inquiry and struggle. Teachers like Eliot allow learners to transform their perspectives about themselves, G*d, religious tradition, and the relationship between the three. The outcome is unpredictable and ongoing, but what remains is developmentally and theologically appropriate for the contemporary cultural circumstances.

Teaching religion responsibly today includes the possibility of deconversion where a religiousness does remain. In the case of this teacher-learner pair, the outcome is not a narcissistic rejection of tradition. Michael does not believe he has all the answers. Nor does he think he can discover them all on his own. The religious dimension of Michael's life reflects a commitment to ongoing critical reflection, openness to other views, and a deepening relationship with the divine.

In an earlier interview, when explaining what he hoped to learn from speaking with his former student, Eliot shared, "If all Michael remembers is that I was a model of faith and he respects me and faith because of it, I'll take it." In truth, Michael learned more than that, but did so because of Eliot's approach. When I asked Eliot whether Michael's religious education had been successful, he and Michael smiled at each other—comfortably. Eliot nodded without hesitation: "You gotta put this one in the win column."

The quality of trust and engagement between these two religious men embodies the promise of religious education, but also its inspiring—or Spirit-filled—unpredictability. Michael has not stopped thinking about the Catholic tradition taught to him by Eliot, among others. In many ways it was the critical reflective process modeled by teachers like Eliot that prepared him to step out onto the waters of the world in which he lives, and to live the sense of tradition he learned in innovating ways.

chapter 3

THE DOER AND THE MYSTIC

Early in the research, I spoke with one potential participant who was explicitly uninterested in the primary focus of the study. According to this religious educator, she "hasn't lost a student in thirty years." Interesting. Her comment represents the contested conversation and narrative of deficiency that surrounds disaffiliation. (It is also statistically unlikely.) Unfortunately, I did not invite this educator to participate because she did not fit the criteria of the study. According to her, she had no former students who now had an ambiguous or disaffiliated relationship with the Catholic Church. I mention her because the portrait and conversation the reader will witness in this chapter represents a similar starting point—if I had begun with the affiliated educator.

On the recommendation of a colleague, I met to discuss the study with Jackie, a young teacher and Catholic school graduate who is now a disaffiliating Catholic. She easily named an extremely formative religious educator during her time in high school. When I located Theresa, the educator that Jackie had named, she had no recollection of the former student. Like the potential participant just mentioned, Theresa might have responded to my invitation to participate in much the same way. On more than one occasion, Theresa had shared with me her negative views of young people leaving the Church. She chose to participate in the study because she loves talking about teaching and was curious whether she would remember her former student when they met. The individual interviews and conversation between Jackie and Theresa provides similar insights on a faithful but critical praxis that can be handed in contemporary teaching-learning relationships. Their conversation also offers a distinct theological reflection and gendered experience of religious learning and disaffiliation. The encounter between these two women was tense at times. The affiliated religious educator in this pair could not put the teaching-learning experience in the "win column," but her response still has much to teach other religious educators in and beyond Catholicism. Theresa also could not ignore the active and meaningful life her former student was living, and how her teaching may have contributed to its form and practice.

AN INITIAL SKETCH

Jackie and Theresa are very different. Frankly, the more I learned about them, the more uncertain I was how the final group interview might go. Anxious actually. Both women were born and raised in Brooklyn. So, diversity is to be expected. Jackie, a young activist and social studies teacher, does not attend church and is very critical of the Catholic institution and questions the existence of G*d. Theresa, her former teacher, asserted that the "spiritual but not religious thing is crap." She also shared her blunt view that "Catholicism is the best religion," and that she wanted all her students to remain affiliated. You can imagine my concern.

These core distinctions accompanied other differences in style and appearance. I first met Jackie near downtown Brooklyn in the hip café she suggested. While transcribing the interview, I was often distracted by how good the background music was. She is in her late twenties, with a little salt and pepper in her hair. Jackie is a runner, shops at Trader Joe's, and dresses with a Brooklyn style. She wore a long fitted coat and wrapped scarf when we first met. I was glad I wore one of my cooler outfits to work that day. Theresa gives an altogether different but nonetheless striking impression of being unbothered by vanity. As we spoke, our conversations were animated and meaningful as she ignored details like the crumbs down her rugged flannel shirts and her somewhat unruly hair. When speaking with Theresa, I felt compelled to unbutton my top button and untuck my shirt to be similarly liberated.

Like Michael in the previous portrait, Jackie is explicitly unsure she has left Catholicism. Despite her criticism and position in relation to the institutional Church, she feels called by aspects of her sense of Catholic tradition. A refrain that emerged during our conversations was the dissonance she feels between the conventional Catholicism presented to her by her family and elements of her all-girls school education that was amazing, open, feminist, social justice focused, and spiritual; she was not rejecting that.

What kept her stuck possibly on one side of the boundary separating the recognizably religious from disaffiliation was the conventional, patriarchal institution that does not treat women as equals. Jackie's sense of Catholic tradition continues to form who she is, what she does, and why she does it. However, she does not believe "there is a Catholic Church that exists where she would fit." Jackie described her family as a significant influence in this regard. She also named Theresa's class on "Women in Christian Tradition" as a "gateway" to the form of Catholicism with which she is comfortable and to a worldview that resonates with her life. Jackie spoke excitedly about the fact that Theresa had somehow disguised a women's studies class as a religious education course. She described how radical it was compared to her other religious education classes. This sounded like an educator I wanted to work with. But finding Theresa proved to be a little difficult.

Finding and contacting Theresa included tracking where else she had taught, pursuing an obituary lead, and many phone calls to her former principals. I learned that she was very much alive and had retired in 2016. When she responded to my invitations to speak on the phone, Theresa was clearly hesitant to speak with such a persistent stranger. However, once we began speaking of teaching, her reticence disappeared. At many points in our conversations, my notes indicated how much she enjoyed speaking of teaching. At one point my field notes state, "It appears at times she is floating above her seat." If we teach who we are, Theresa is earthy, authentic, deeply spiritual, and irreverent. I have a feeling she was a challenge to Catholic school administrators.

Theresa shared with me details of her difficult life history from which a charismatic Catholic faith saved her—not once, but twice. Her story is not intellectual or typical. Though she did earn an MA in theology, the faith she developed is raw and mostly self-taught through prayer. Although affiliation is important to her, she is utterly unconventional, anti-authority, and very loving. Though her blunt comments can suggest the opposite, suspending judgment emerged as a significant part of her teaching practice and theology. Theresa's goal in her teaching is affiliation. However, her more ultimate hope for her students is that they develop a habit of theological reflection, and come to know G*d's incarnate love.

As the final interview approached, another reason for my concern was that even after some attempts to remind her, Theresa did not remember Jackie. Theresa does present as a kind of absent-minded professor. Often during our conversations she forgot words necessary to complete a sentence, but not necessary to complete her thought. Such details never derailed her from the idea she was communicating. It was thrilling at times to follow her thoughts and communication of spirituality. She often appeared to forget I was there. That she truly had no recollection of her former student was a real possibility. Moreover, although I explained the focus of the study and the reason for the group conversation, Theresa did not seem to acknowledge that her former student was not an affiliated Catholic anymore. It was her complete trust and lack of concern that concerned me.

MEETING JACKIE

I found Jackie on the recommendation of a colleague—her mother—who explained that while religion is so important to her, it is not so for her daughter. However, the mother admitted that she struggles with her own religious identity, so wonders if she has any right to expect her daughter to affiliate. Jackie's mother volunteered that her daughter might be religious without expressing it institutionally. She noted that her daughter's commitment to social justice and education is substantial and life giving. These two themes indeed do structure and give meaning to life for the young woman I met.

Jackie has been teaching eighth-grade social studies at an all-girls urban charter school for six years. Jackie spoke with an emotional range and intelligence I associate with teachers. Tears came comfortably during our conversation when speaking of her grandmother who had recently passed away. Jackie also laughed easily, at her own jokes more than at mine. (It was the better choice. She is very funny.) She twisted her hair in thought as she listened to questions and as she replied, often expressing thoughts she had never before tried to articulate. Jackie clearly enjoys this kind of reflection and conversation. Our first conversation ended a little early because we were being motioned out of the trendy coffee shop where we were meeting. As we were packing up, Jackie said, "Wow. That was great. We can go longer next time. I've got lots more."

Though teaching occupies most of Jackie's time, she gets up early to indulge in one of her hobbies: after skimming the local morning papers, she writes a very smart and humorous digest email with links to the major stories and sends it to her friends, family, and one researcher. When Jackie is not at school, she is usually planning curriculum. On the weekends, she guards her time to be with friends, her boyfriend, and herself. Jackie explained that running has become a new meditative time for her. She lives with her boyfriend who is also a runner, and who was also "raised Catholic." They go for a run together on the weekend, cook a lot together, and socialize with college friends who live nearby. What matters most in Jackie's typical week is teaching and spending time with her boyfriend. Though religion is a significant part of her family history and identity, she does not attend church and is not sure where she fits in the discussion of religion.

> I don't really know how I identify religiously right now. I'm not sure if that's a good answer . . . but I've definitely told people that I feel like I am culturally Catholic, if that makes sense. . . . Growing up I just always knew both my parents were Catholic.

Jackie's grandfather is an Eastern Rite Catholic priest, her aforementioned mother is a professor of religion at a Catholic university, her father is one of ten siblings, and her parents met as Jesuit volunteers. That said, her family "is not a conservative group of people by any means, but they are very much a group of Catholic people. . . . So it's just always been in the background." Jackie grew up going to Mass with her family in the church where she was baptized. When her parents divorced at six years old, her mother began taking her sister and Jackie to a different church. Mass became something she did with her mom and sister. Jackie did not go when she was staying with her dad. Although her father was distancing himself from the Church, that was not an option for her. Jackie recalled, "Even if I had friends over, they would come with us." Although she experienced Mass as a chore, Jackie explained she never tried to get out of going.

> It's funny . . . I pushed back on a lot of stuff. . . . I was talking to this woman I work with who was telling a story about the first time she refused to go to church. . . . I never would have tried to pull that . . . I would have felt guilty. . . . Mass just felt like part of our family schedule. I probably would have also felt guilty for refusing to eat dinner with my mom or grandmother.

Growing up, Jackie identified as Catholic and thought she "believed all those things we are supposed to." It was what everyone in her family did. Her family's parish was not conservative, and she does not remember hearing a homily that sent her running for the door. Neither her parish, nor her family were "fire and brimstone kind of Catholics." She did, however, recall feeling disconnected to such a male-dominated place. It was in high school that Jackie's relationship with the church started changing.

In her all-girls Catholic high school, Jackie first began imagining alternatives as she was encouraged to think about religion in her theology courses. "There were certainly things I learned where I was like, 'NOooo!' What's funny, though, is there were also things I started to appreciate more about Catholicism [by] being in an all-girls environment." The experience of women in the church and her experience as a woman in her Catholic all-women high school represents an ongoing tension for Jackie that keeps her both connected and outside the church's institutional influence. Her grandmother's example, aspects of her school experience, and Theresa's class inspired her with a more expansive view of Catholic tradition but they do not completely overcome her experiences of conventional Catholicism as exclusive, alienating, and oppressive.[1]

Jackie praised the fact that in her high school experience most of the authority figures were women, but . . .

> I will never forget sitting in my history class the first day of ninth grade. The teacher wrote on the board "H-I-S-t-o-r-y" and put a box around H-I-S and explained history was G*d's story, HIS story. I was like, "What the hell is going on?" I also remember a teacher had us watch a video of an abortion. . . . That was where I started to think this was not for me. If this is what this is about, I'm not buying what you're selling.

In hindsight, she realizes that her high school may have only given "lip service" to women's leadership, but no one communicated that at the time to Jackie, or Theresa, who took them at their word.

Coupled with this institutional dilemma regarding gender in the church, the question of G*d stirred doubts in young Jackie. Although identifying as an atheist would have been very scary for her to say out loud then, she admitted that more recently she might have taken on that title. When they started dating, her boyfriend was a "loud and proud atheist." However, they share similar views today. Jackie hesitated to identify as atheist even during those times it might have made sense because she thinks doing so

---

1. See Winter et al., *Defecting in Place*. The study reports that 81 percent of laywomen and 82 percent of religious women feel angry and alienated with the institutional church. They experience the church to be "exclusive and oppressive, demeaning and humiliating, violating and out of touch." Winter et al. give a compelling description of one form of deconversion without using that language. "Defecting in Place" suggests leaving old affiliations and ways of relating but staying on one's own terms. Their book describes women who have created and participate in small feminist prayer groups where they feel they can more authentically belong.

would give the impression that she has dismissed everything about religion. This is not who, or where, she is. Jackie is unsure of her theology but is comforted in and through elements of Catholic tradition.

"Have I Left Catholicism?": The Deconversion Process

As our conversations moved naturally from her childhood to her religious life now, Jackie emoted pleasant and intrigued surprise that she continued to return to the paradoxical position that "I don't think I have 'left' Catholicism . . . I am just not interested in what is being presented in the churches that exist." Jackie in many ways is emblematic of the research reviewed in chapter one. Her significant community involvement, personal growth practices, and emphasis on service complicate reductive views of less-than-affiliated religiousness. She does not reject tradition, and she does not convey a self-concerned individualism. Whether Jackie is a "None" or a "Some" is one of the questions we explored, and whether that language was helpful at all. She certainly lives with and organizes her life by what some might consider "religious" concerns. Jackie herself admits as such, but hesitantly.

Her experiences of religious education in high school and college allowed Jackie to say some of the things she felt unsure of saying out loud as a child. "When I went to college, I felt like no one is making me do this . . . so at that point . . . I wanted to be on my own." At college and on her own, Jackie was exposed to diverse worldviews, people, and opportunities. These opportunities included the elements of Catholic tradition that spoke to her, and where she felt she fit. Jackie was active in College Democrats, and became very involved in service learning opportunities in her community.

> There was a center on campus that ran all these different classes you could either take or facilitate. I did both. Most of the ones I did were in a jail. I would go once a week to a jail and teach writing programs there. I did it both as a student and as a facilitator. That was a place where I felt like I fit. This is cool. I get this. . . . I did it my first semester and I really liked it. . . . I probably felt like I should be doing something like that . . . thinking about the social justice components of Catholicism. I think at the time I would have been reluctant to admit that . . . but I do think that was probably a driving force.

Jackie's experiences in active service and in the few churchgoing experiences during this time crystallized for her how and what Catholicism she "practiced." Her college roommate for all four years, and still a close friend, was raised Methodist and attended a very large evangelical church. When Jackie attended services with her roommate, she was shocked at the church's size, sound, and emphasis on personal redemption.

> I remember thinking, I know I am not sure I understand where I come from, but I really don't understand this. And if I do believe in anything, it's certainly not this. . . . That was when I started to think about how I would identify as a Catholic person, if I decided to do that. It would be because of the acts of Catholicism. . . . Not that I think other denominations don't do acts of service, but I feel like I can say this because it's anonymous . . . to me, Jesuit Catholicism, true social-justice Catholicism, . . . "gets it" in a way that I don't think a lot of other faiths do. I appreciate that kind of Catholicism because I saw it in my grandmother. Your religion is not your personal belief in G*d. It's the way you are serving others. That's what I appreciated about my grandmother, the Jesuit Volunteer corps, Catholic charities, and Catholic relief services. That is where I could see myself fitting in it. . . . When I think about being Catholic, what that means, when I see it in a way I can connect with, that is what I see.

Jackie's dedication to social justice is clear in her professional choices and is what motivates her as a teacher in urban schools. Her relationship with G*d, or questions concerning that relationship, continue as well. She shared about her long tradition of going into Catholic churches and lighting candles and thinking of her grandmother, even before she died. She explained a recent change in that practice that involved not simply "thinking nice thoughts" but praying a Hail Mary. Jackie was not sure why she started doing so, but she was certain that she liked it. She accepted this new habit as indicative of her affinity for the rituals of Catholicism to communicate and comfort human experience.

"Why Is It So Hard for a Woman to Be Recognized?": For the Sake of Authenticity

Jackie's grandmother was a focus of our conversations. She had died a few months earlier and her funeral services were Jackie's last experiences in a church. Her grandmother was and is an important figure in her life. Jackie explained how she had found comfort in the structure of the funeral liturgy and appreciated that it is a tool to work through and express grief, but also to celebrate a life. She shared that her grandmother's parents had died when she was very young, that she had gone on to graduate college with a degree in chemistry, had had eleven children, and given endlessly to mostly Catholic service organizations and causes. Jackie attributed her own focus on social justice and service to her grandmother, and explained that her grandmother was a core reason why she associates action with being Catholic more than anything else. "I think about it a lot, and . . . I wonder if I should be giving more. Obviously in terms of time too, not just money. I am a teacher, so I am not a millionaire. . . . But since last year, I've been trying to give more money away."

In her family, Jackie's grandmother was a model of female Catholic leadership. Jackie explained that the homily given by her grandmother's pastor was clear about the leadership roles and responsibilities her grandmother held and performed in her community. Then:

> This is where I really get stuck. . . . Why is it so hard for her to be recognized? Why did she have to give all her money away to be recognized? I know you can't separate these two things. My grandmother was driven by her faith to do all the great things she did . . . but she was driven to do all that good by an institution that told her she was not an equal. I think part of what's keeping me from identifying as Catholic is that it's such a male hierarchy that I don't feel any connection to, nor do I believe in it. . . . Which is why I say I am culturally Catholic.

Like many in her position, Jackie struggled with language to describe her current practices and beliefs. She emphasized that she does not believe in many of the things that some Catholics believe in. She highlighted Paul Ryan and Pope Benedict as examples of conventional Catholicism that, among other things, is "Pro-life until birth" and that she would be loath to be associated with. She was hopeful about Pope Francis but unconvinced. She commented a few times that people gave him too much credit. "He could and should be doing more." Despite these criticisms of the Catholic institution, she does not use language of "spiritual but not religious" to describe her religious identity. "I think if I was searching for more of the G*d part, I might say I am 'spiritual,' but I identify with the active part." Jackie clarified that there is spirituality to her actions, but she does not use the world "spiritual" or "spirituality." We commiserated on the problem of language regarding these more fluid positions and identities. I offered a list of contemporary possible categories such as "None," "Some," "Lapsed,"

"Former," "Deconvert" (she looked a little bemused at that one; I would have followed up to explain the term but she reacted strongly to the last category I shared) and "Secular Catholic."[2]

> Interesting. I like that idea of Secular Catholic . . . but I would be reluctant to use it because there's a lot of baggage that comes with what people think of when they hear the word "Catholic," both Catholic and non-Catholic people. There are so many historic things that are wrong with the church that I don't feel connected to and wouldn't want to imply that I feel connected to those things. But I like "secular Catholicism," because that kind of gets you honest. My mom is kind of living there too, even though she is a professor of religion. My dad also. He considered converting to Buddhism four or five years ago but has a large picture of Mary in his bedroom. I don't think that would make a lot of sense to a lot of people, but it makes sense to me. . . . So, have I left Catholicism? I am not sure.

We laughed together at this for we agreed that this was the significance of the current study: A lot of people are indeed "living there" and it does "make sense" to some, but not to others.

"The Pronoun Thing Blew My Mind": A Renewed Sense of Divine Presence

One significant lesson Jackie learned growing up was that you were supposed to go to church. If you did not attend Mass, you were guilty of something. As a child, she believed in a G*d who could hear all her thoughts. She recalled this belief as mostly positive, but also negative—and this led her to sharing stories of having to go to confession. Jackie remembered having to make up sins like cheating on homework and being mean to her sister just to have something to say. Then she would feel bad for lying! The lesson learned was she had to be better at being bad.

With these childhood religious education memories, Jackie was not surprised by many of the Catholic elements of her high school. She

---

2. Tom Beaudoin uses this term to describe Catholics in the United States today that do not attend Mass regularly, disagree with church teachings, and do not make Catholicism the center of their lives, at least not Catholicism as it is interpreted by official Church teachings. Many continue to think of themselves in relationship to Catholicism, but that relationship is outside of normative Catholicism. See Beaudoin, "Secular Catholicism and Practical Theology."

mentioned more than once her experience on her first day of class when her teacher explained that history was H-I-S-Story as one example of the conventional Catholicism present at the school. She also shared a story of her physics teacher daring the class to think of a profession that did not use physics. So she asked, "What if you want to be a nun?" Jackie's teacher made her the prayer leader of the class as punishment for her comment. Jackie's religious education courses were unfortunately similar—except for one class.

In the ninth grade, Jackie studied Scripture. She remembered that the priest who taught the class would have rather taught another subject. In sophomore year, Jackie studied church history. "I don't remember a single thing we learned in it . . . except it was taught by a spacey older guy who . . . would always start class by asking if anyone had any intentions to pray for. People took extreme advantage of that. . . . We'd say Hail Marys for sick dogs." In junior year, Jackie's teacher taught Morality, maybe.

> The teacher gave us a test once where a question was, "A gay bash is a party homosexuals attend. True or False." The girl in front of me had chosen the wrong answer. I thought to myself, "This is a morality class, should I tap her on the shoulder and let her cheat off my test? That feels like the moral thing to do in this case."

With my own mouth agape and eyes wide, I shared with Jackie that I would use this scenario as a discussion prompt the next time I teach ethics. In that class, Jackie also recalled having to watch a lot of Lifetime movies on abortion, cloning, and dating. Her description of these courses gave me the impression her religious life now might be very different if these had been her only exposure to Catholic tradition. I wondered whether she would have any interest in Catholicism at all?

Jackie remembered her senior year more clearly because she had electives and was able to attend Theresa's class called "Women in the Christian Tradition." It was only a semester, however. The second half of senior year she took another class from the same teacher who taught Morality. It was called Marriage and the Family. Taught in an all-girl's school, by a man, the class was about keeping a household budget and deciding when to get married. Jackie remembered much more about Theresa's class because she learned something that changed how she saw herself and the world.

> I remember the first thing she did was that she talked about how if G*d is this being that is not human, there is no reason for us to only be using male pronouns to describe G*d. I was like What!?'

> But it made a lot of sense to me. . . . It seems like she tricked the school into letting her teach a women's studies 101 course under the guise of a religion class. . . . I remember reading an article about prostitution happening in New Jersey, but the article's perspective wasn't like this was bad and these women are doing a bad thing. We were talking about it more like, why is this is a situation that occurs for some women? . . . But, you know, we did religious stuff too. . . . I would love to look at the readings we did again. . . . I wonder if my mom still has my notebook. . . . I remember more from that class than I do from any other religion class. . . . That pronoun thing blew my mind.

Although Jackie had begun to question whether she believed in G*d at all during high school, she recalled thinking that "I could get into G*d the way [Theresa] talked about G*d." None of her other religion classes impacted her beyond further diminishing her interest in Catholicism. But Theresa's course, and how she taught its content, made a lasting impression that has manifested in Jackie's life in tangible ways. Jackie explained, "I had been raised Catholic my whole life, and the thought never crossed my mind! We could talk about G*d as a She! . . . It wasn't like she was teaching anything that I hadn't been taught before, but she was just framing it in new way." One refrain that emerged in our conversations was how powerful it was for Jackie to have those kinds of reframing and disruptive conversations in a Catholic environment where everyone speaking was a woman.

MEETING THERESA

I met Theresa not far from the school where she had taught Jackie. Old painted and neon signs above the few cafés remaining in the working-class neighborhood revealed its Italian roots. Now the young people skateboarding past the men playing bocce are Asian, Latino, and Eastern European. Walking to meet Theresa, I was aware of the forces and factors of change in her world—including culture and class. The standard decor of the well-known coffee shop where we met was amended with Chinese visual accents, and everyone was speaking Mandarin.

Theresa arrived wearing rugged jeans, boots, and a flannel shirt. She wore eyeglasses with rainbow flags on the sides, and her eyes were not yet certain of me. Her serious presentation thawed quickly into an easily-excited and easy-to-laugh manner. Simply asking about her experiences and goals as a teacher transformed her posture and affect. Theresa has a way of getting carried away with an idea. I could imagine her commanding a classroom by the simple fact that her students would hang on every word she said, unsure of what she was going to say or do next.

Theresa admitted, and in our final interview the three of us agreed as teachers, that setting students up for shock and awe is part of the craft—a trade secret really for those who can do it well. I think of Jesus the Teacher who used shocking and suggestive parables to prepare those listening for his teachings. When it comes to teaching religion, you do first have to contend with the conventional religion to which your learners have become accustomed. They expect more of the same. They listen with a different part of their brains when they realize their teacher is different and old assumptions no longer apply. Theresa explained that she enjoys this part of teaching. "I have always been, how do you say . . . a ham! I don't mind making a fool of myself." She explained that she would use this gift to draw her students out of narrow views of the world, the church, and of women.

In our conversations, Theresa shared what at first seemed an inconsistent declaration. She claimed that her students remaining affiliated with the Catholic Church was absolutely important to her as a teacher, but she also explained that her ultimate hope was to develop in her students a habit of theological reflection and that she "wanted no control over where it led." Theresa trusts G*d acts in that practice and relationship to lead learners to the Spirit, as it did her.

"I Really Wanted to Shock Them": A Religious Educational Style

As a young student, Theresa thought teachers must be out of their minds to choose their profession. She admitted early and happily how wrong she was that teaching was doing the same thing, day in, day out, for years. "In my experience, every single year I learned something new and different, something wonderful and frightening, and scary"—because she was never the same, and neither were her students. As a teacher, Theresa would bring in new things she was reading. She noted that even reading the same Scripture passage was never the same because she would hear it differently depending on the students with whom she was learning. Theresa loved that her students showed her new things in passages she thought she knew inside and out.

The Doer and The Mystic

Theresa taught religion for thirty-four years at all-girls Catholic high schools. As an educator, she was largely self-taught, having taken only a few education courses. As a result, according to Theresa, her first years of teaching were difficult. "In those first four years, I was either going to make it, or be broken by it." She shared a story of her worst moment teaching:

> It was maybe my second or third year teaching. I was trying to explain there are different ways people communicate. It was the 1980s and you had the kids in California saying things like, "Oh my God, gag me with a spoon." I was using that as an example. One girl opened up, "Oh yeah. I love that," and she started sharing to the class. But I told her, "Talking like that is so ridiculous."
>
> I watched it right then. The light went out of her eyes. Damn. I swore from that moment on, I would not make that mistake again. I lost her for the rest of the year . . . I lost her by judging her. By not listening. I could have said, anything else. "Yeah, that is interesting . . ." and she would have been on board.

Theresa, seeming to forget I was there, looked up, and recalled the many times in her teaching career after that moment when she suspended her judgment of an idea or of one of her students. Instead, she developed the teaching habit of asking questions. She shared excitedly, "Then I would learn something myself because, obviously, they are looking at things from a different perspective than I am. . . . It has been a long, strange trip, as the Grateful Dead would say. It has obviously been my calling. I just didn't know it early on."

As we talked, Theresa shared with me her course through her early career when she learned more and about "her craft" and improved at it by "thinking about what better questions I should ask?" With experience, she learned what would work and what would not. She would alter course and, when needed, create something new that would work. This conversation about her creative teaching process reminded her of the course she had created for seniors, the one about which I was most curious: "Women in the Christian Tradition."

When I asked about the origins of this class, Theresa spoke of a community college professor who inspired her as a student with his gift of drawing together seemingly disparate elements to determine patterns and meaning. She explained that from that moment, she wanted to teach like that and connect religion with the world in which her students were living. "I really believe G*d gave me that gift to be able to see things and how they fit together."

The idea for the Women in Christian Tradition course came from that desire and from looking at her sister's collection of women's magazines.

> I used to look through them, and think, "What the hell is going on here?" That was the beginning of the course that I didn't know that I was creating. I started collecting these magazine pictures and tried to figure out what they seemed to be saying about me as a woman, and to girls. That was one part of it. And then the light shone—it was all about the Incarnation. That Jesus Christ is a human being. He's bodily, so what does bodyliness mean for men? What does it mean for women? . . . It really took me a couple years of teaching it to recognize that all cultures, in some way . . . create the female body, tell you what is good and bad, cut the body, cover the body, or in our culture, uncover the body.

The class began with identifying stereotypes and asked students what it might mean to be a unified and integrative person. Theresa shared honestly that the reactions of her students to the content of the course and to her shocking teaching style were mixed. Jackie echoed this observation, explaining that sometimes her fellow students did not know how to respond to their teacher. Theresa and Jackie both independently mentioned that many of her students thought Theresa must have been a nun or something. "Students would often ask me, 'Where do you come from?'" Theresa admitted. "I am a bit different." She explained her unorthodox approach:

> I just wanted them to know the love of G*d. That is why I acted like that . . . I really wanted to shock them. That was really what I wanted to do. I wanted them to walk away with, "Oh my g*d! You're a religion teacher. You're not supposed to say those things." To which I would say, "Yet I am."

Theresa explained that the purpose of her shock and awe teaching campaigns were to provoke conversations that would "open doors and windows to let new thoughts come in." There was a learning curve for her as a teacher for determining how much challenge was helpful.

Theresa shared curriculum materials that demonstrated her goals of presenting and wrestling with controversial and complex material like the rape culture, racism, and heterosexism. In her classroom conversations regarding the church's teachings on homosexuality, she subtly challenged the church's position by pointing out the rhetorical sleight of hand often used to approve discrimination. Separating the expression of homosexuality as sinful but the person as worthy of love is impossible, Theresa explained. She had a saying that "all human beings deserve love and justice for the mere fact that they are made in the image of G*d." She would add, "People are whole. And we are not here to judge, but to take care of people, and live in justice. All human beings are due that."

What became clear is that Theresa loved teaching. When I asked her what she remembered most, she glanced away and her eyes got that transported look: "I just remember the laughter. We talked to each other." Theresa explained that her greatest hope for her students was that they develop a habit and practice of reflection. "I most certainly don't want any control over where they take that reflection. I just hope they take it with them." She expressed a basic and sustaining faith that when a person opens their imagination, G*d enters in. "God reaches down and pulls you up. So that is my greatest hope."

One intriguing assignment she described demonstrated this hope and her efforts to hand it on to her students. Theresa had sophomore girls put a penny in their shoe for week, and carry one line from scripture in their pockets. She asked the girls to read the passage every morning and night, and reflect in the journal on what it meant to them. During the day, they were to recite and reflect on the passage each time they felt the penny. "A lot of them thought it was annoying. Maybe that isn't a bad thing, I told them . . . creating a habit of thinking about G*d in their lives." Listening to Theresa describe her courses and such unique activities, it was clear that she misses teaching.

Theresa shared the difficulty she was having in retirement. Her decision to retire stemmed from her school administration making some decisions that she felt were counter to its religious mission. Theresa resisted the temptation to speak more of that relationship. In a mischievous smile, I sensed the common tension that exists between radical religious educators and those charged with keeping the lights on in religious institutions. When I asked Theresa, "If it's true we teach who we are, who are you as a teacher?" she hesitated, unsure of how her response might be received, and asked to pass on that question. When I returned home, I had received an email explaining her reticence:

> I was ruminating on the question you asked that I had a hard time answering: If we teach who we are, who are you as a teacher? . . . The idea that came to mind was that I am the Incarnation, or that is what I try to be with all my might. It is only through the power of G*d's grace that I am. I get to feel some of that energy—the Holy

> Spirit—coursing through my human veins and in my heart, mind, and soul. And I just follow it. . . . Is that blasphemous? Am I being truly irreverent? We are all called to be the Incarnation, are we not?

She is right, and on good theological footing. However, the church's history certainly does include punishing women with similar ideas. Theresa has lived, learned, and now teaches from this rebellious, alternative, and deeply spiritual tradition within the Catholic tradition.

"Found My Way Back to the Spirit": A Conversion

Theresa was raised in a mixed Catholic and convert household. Her father became Catholic when he married her mom. Theresa tried on a few different words to try to describe her family before settling on: "We didn't say I love you a lot or hug each other, that kind of thing." This stern and expressionless family environment set young Theresa apart.

> At maybe eleven or twelve, I remember opening Christmas presents. . . . You know as a kid you are usually thinking, "Is there more. Is there anything more?" I remember starting to think about what this life is for. Why are we here? That kind of thing, while opening presents. I think that was the first little snippet of when I started to think about Jesus, and that we are here to love others. I remember feeling what a great thing it is to have my sister and my mother and my father. I have always remembered that beginning. . . . I also remember at the same time my grandmother started telling me, "Windy,[3] stop thinking so deeply." I didn't think I was thinking too deeply. I was just trying to explain the things that were happening inside me.

Theresa has a twin sister, but noted that growing up her sister had friends whereas Theresa did not fit in with any crowd. When her Catholic grammar school was going make her repeat a grade for daydreaming, her parents sent both Theresa and her sister to public school. Theresa explained it was the best thing that could have happened to her. The new school had art programs, music programs, theater, and gym class. She has always been more of a hands-on and kinesthetic learner. The real reason that she liked going to church as child, she admitted, was that she got to sing. (She still sings and paints large religious art pieces that are quite stunning and visual representations of her

---

3. Theresa has a childhood nickname she still uses. This is a pseudonym of that handle that tries to mirror its natural and spiritual connotations.

deep and evolving spirituality.) In the seventh and eighth grades, however, she and her sister had to be bussed to a different school where gang intimidation and recruitment was common. Those years were traumatizing for Theresa. One day she stepped in to stand up for a fellow seventh grader being picked on by a sophomore and junior. For the rest of her time at that school she had to be walked to the bus by the assistant principal. "Students were always trying to jump me . . . I was afraid all the time."

Theresa did not find a community where she fit in until her freshmen year of high school when her sister took her to her first charismatic prayer group. She does not remember how her sister found it, but it became something she and her sister did together. Theresa attended the group all four years of high school. The group included Franciscan Capuchin friars, lay people of all ages, and persons with various spiritual gifts. Theresa shared about one young woman whose life was terribly traumatic that would speak, through the Spirit, as Jesus himself. She recalled that while this woman channeled Jesus, she would speak to the group like they were his children about both the joy and the suffering of this life. It made a lasting impression on Theresa concerning what prayer is, and what church is.

The prayer group brought her closer with her sister, and ultimately her family. Theresa's parents attended a similar group. On occasion, she did attend her parents' meeting where the spiritual gifts included speaking in tongues and healings through prayer. The gathering involved a simple structure of lay-led Bible reflection. Theresa now leads a similar group called ARISE whose goal is to create more of these small communities of prayer. She shared that despite this formative experience during her teenage years, her churchgoing ended abruptly during her twenties. When I asked what prompted the change, Theresa slowed her speech to share about a dark period in her life.

Theresa then spoke again of her philosophy instructor in community college who showed her the way she wanted to teach, a way that at the time felt utterly out of reach. She explained again his gift for drawing together seemingly disparate things from life to reveal a pattern. Theresa was inspired. She decided teaching was what she wanted to do with her life. "That's what I want to be able to do. I want to be able to see the connectedness in life." But when she tried, it felt beyond her intellectual reach. "I fell into a depression because, for a moment, I had an idea for my life—then I lost it." She hesitantly confessed that the people she was spending time with, and "the drugs, alcohol, and so on" also likely influenced the darkness.

> I don't want to blame my husband.... We started going out when he was eighteen years old. I am three years older than he is.... He was going to be a priest. I guess part of his breaking away was drinking, smoking, and spending time with frightening guys with guns. I started hanging out with him and his friends. They were nice guys, but they were pretty heavy drug users, a lot of alcohol, a lot of pornography. I allowed myself to get drawn into that world and I convinced myself that this was part of being a human being. That I had been too long up in the divine and that I really didn't know what it was to be a human being. I thought, "This is what I should participate in." I don't know how I got that idea. I became lost, suicidal even.

During this period, Theresa never thought she had left Catholicism. She just felt sad. "The kind of sorrow that feels like you could never come back," she explained. "I had immersed myself in a hedonism that led to nothing but darkness.... My husband felt the same way." Theresa played a little guitar, not well she said, but she expressed her gratitude for this persistent interest that helped her "find her way back to the Spirit."

When Theresa decided to start taking lessons, her guitar teacher suggested she play at a local church. When she did, she began singing with the folk group. Theresa developed friendships and returned to weekly Mass attendance. What ultimately brought her back to life was a great pastor:

> He was a soft-spoken, prayerful man. During confession when I was explaining where I was coming from, he said, "you're kind of like the prodigal son." At first, I was like, "I am not like the prodigal son. Who do you think you are talking to!?" Then I was like, "Oh my G*d. I *am* the prodigal son. It was a wake-up call."

While she was returning to full and active church participation, Theresa was also working toward an MA in theology. Her experience in academia was not completely satisfying. She felt the theology presented by her professors leaned too far into the humanity of Jesus and came close to denying his divinity. She envisioned a more integrative view, and grew from this theology toward her own "creative path of following G*d" by pursuing the "freedom Christ provides." Theresa developed this theology on her own through years of prayer. "I saw the Divine, matter, and the Spirit together. I wanted to share that freedom with my students."

Immediately after graduation, Theresa began teaching. She was frank in her description of those first years teaching, "I was just horrible. I would come home crying every day. 'I don't want to do this.'" It was then another formative teacher appeared. Theresa explained that her professor at a local seminary demonstrated to her that before you can draw connections between diverse elements of everyday life, you have to build a basic structure, a container to house the ideas you intend to stir up and reorganize. "Once you have the structure, then you can add all the color and extras." Theresa remembered this professor for both the structure he provided and humorous way he added controversy and challenge. "From there I began to find my way, the next three years were still a struggle to teach . . . but by the end of the fourth year, I had it."

Theresa paused the story of her early teaching experiences as she decided it was pertinent to share that despite this success, the mid 1980s were still a hard time for her. She begged my pardon for the change of subject but explained that this dramatic experience had made a lasting impact on her life.

> When my twin sister got married, they learned that they weren't able to have children. My sister and her husband decided to adopt a child from a place in the Ukraine. In the process, my sister got pregnant. But because she had had so much trouble becoming pregnant, the doctors told her shouldn't travel to pick up their adopted daughter. They asked me to go with her husband. At that point a friend of mine had just died from AIDS. It was a horrible, horrible, death. I'd never seen anything like that. I had never been there while someone was dying. I looked at this trip as a chance to find new life, so I went.
>
> We took a sixteen-hour plane ride to Ukraine. It was the Russian Orthodox Easter. We arrived on Good Friday. At the orphanage they kept telling us this could all fall apart at any moment and we couldn't take her home. We waited. It was my brother-in-law and me, and this other woman who also adopting a child. It was like a sweetness out of the darkness. The three of us in the upper room, having dinner and talking about how we got there, our lives, our beliefs. Saturday passed with no word. And then on Sunday, we went to pick up Karyn. . . . It was like one of those mystical things you never plan on. . . . I held her in my arms, this beautiful, gorgeous little child. It was a wonderfully healing thing. . . . We brought her home. That was one of those wonderful moments that G*d has given us.

Theresa returned from this retelling resolved all over again, and reminded herself, and me, that it had been quite a journey full of different and difficult experiences that made sense only now. She trusts G*d was with her during all of it, even in the dark times. Theresa suggested she needed to be lost before she could be found. "I absolutely needed to go through all of it to be where I am today."

FINAL PORTRAIT: TEACHING A CREATIVE AND ACTIVE PATH OF FOLLOWING G*D

Jackie explained that while the Catholicism of her high school restrained her in some ways, in other ways she felt safe and empowered by it. She connected this experience to her current motivation as a teacher. Jackie explained how she works to create a safe place for her mostly black female students. "I think about what it means for them to be voters and hope they feel armed with enough information to understand the larger context of anything that is going on so they can make their own informed choices." When I asked Jackie whether she thought her religious education was successful, she gave the question a serious smirk. "Successful at what? Making me a lifelong church attender? No." What it did do, in concert with her family, was help her learn how she wanted to walk in the world. Reflecting more on the idea, Jackie pondered out loud that she might have learned that more from the all-girl environment of her high school than from any one religion class. She explained,

> There is something really powerful about in every room, at any moment, with the exception of male teachers, the person sharing is a woman. The smartest person in the room is going to be a woman. The person who gets the highest grade is going to be a woman. The president of the student council is going to be a woman.... I think it gives you a level of confidence and safety that I want to share with my students also.

Jackie added to this comment that she did not ever want to find herself doing a job she did not think had social value. She is committed to work she feels serves a greater good. "I think that is important for me to live a good and happy life. I don't think I would feel happy if I wasn't in service to others, whatever that means . . . and that is probably a little bit Catholic."

This life mission Jackie articulated is indeed a "little bit Catholic," especially knowing where she learned its value and its "practice." While she agrees that she inherited and learned significant theological views and practices that structure and provide meaning for her life, Jackie is not interested in what she sees in conventional churches. Jackie admits she has a very *active* Catholicity, but does not think she will ever return to churchgoing Catholicism—because she has not lost what is to her the most important element of being Catholic.

When I asked Jackie about the possibility of attending Mass at a parish, she shared that she and her boyfriend sometime joke, "We should go to church this weekend." She confessed this is "kind of joking. Kind of not." Jackie explained that neither she or her boyfriend really want to go to Mass, but they appreciate the comfortable and structured celebration of the values by which they continue to live. Her boyfriend is also active in social justice in their local community personally and professionally. Jackie shared with me that she sees the appeal of going to church, just like she does going for a run with her boyfriend every weekend. However, she could not imagine finding and connecting with a church community because, "I just don't know if that Catholic Church exists." When I asked her what she thought was next in her religious life, she admitted she has been thinking about tangible ways to be connected to Catholicism that would not compromise on the things she definitely does believe or on the things she definitely disagrees with.

When Jackie, Theresa, and I were finally able to coordinate schedules for our final interview, I arrived early. As I reviewed the interview guide I had created, I also had time to revisit my concerns. I was nervous that the differences between this activist and her charismatic teacher might prove too awkward for the conversation to be pleasant. I was worried that Theresa's frank way with words might shame Jackie about her choices to distance herself or depart from conventional Catholicism. Theresa had shared her thoughts with me on disaffiliation among Catholic young adults in her typical manner:

> You mean the people saying that they're not religious but they're spiritual? I think that is crap. . . . I think it's foolish to say that all religious beliefs are all on the same level. [It] would be stupid for me to say: "This is the religion I am following." "Why are you following it?" "Oh, well. I don't know. It's kind of like the rest of them." No . . . I am a Catholic. And I love being a Catholic. It is the best expression of worship of G*d. I would like all Catholics to hold on to that faith.

So, yes . . . I was concerned. However, that said, Theresa was not all criticism when it came to alternative paths of religious life and learning.

Theresa articulated her own troubling experiences and doctrinal dilemmas with the church leadership, not least of all its patriarchy. She shared the constructive and creative path she found out of what she did admit were reasonable issues with the institutional church. Theresa explained she has remained affiliated by following the path of the saints. "Whatever you think about the Catholic Church structure, I look to the saints. The saints are the ones who have always called the structure into question." Theresa spoke of the way of life, and path laid out by these "absurd and diverse people" as they followed G*d in creative ways beyond the socially and ecclesial accepted boundaries. She wondered aloud about who those saints might be today, and whether we would recognize or persecute them. She did not immediately make the connection I did when she said this. I was thinking of active but less-than affiliated Catholics like Jackie. She only nodded when I pointed out the possibility.

Because of my concerns, I decided to enter into our final meeting as more of a conversation participant than interviewer to diffuse any possible judgment that might inadvertently arise. The worry turned out to be for naught. The conversation that occurred in between their two different worlds in Brooklyn was delightful and built on the care and pleasure we each take in the craft of teaching. The conversation expanded from the practice of teaching to explore their particular teaching-learning relationship and how its result fits into what religion might be becoming. In that conversation, Theresa spoke of teaching as a religious activity.

Theresa's teaching style models learning as a sacred process. In the classroom and in our conversation, she implicitly, and at times explicitly, shared graphically her own dark and idiosyncratic spiritual journey. For Theresa, her own exploration, loss, and discovery are more authoritative than any institutional authority. "I understand troubling experiences with conventional religion and not feeling like I fit in," she explained to Jackie. Theresa shared how she has dealt with it using the theatrical and comedic timing of which she had boasted in her teaching. As she stared down and to the left and let her face go slack, she exhaled, "I have dealt with the church's failures with tears, depression, and despair." Then breaking character before the next inhale, "No. Not really. I have dealt with it through prayer, of course. I come back to it constantly, especially when I feel depressed by some of the things that the bishops say or do." Theresa explained again to Jackie that she trusts there are and will be saints that call the church into question and challenge the power it presumes. For

Theresa, this is not an academic perspective. In her teaching and in our conversation, she attempted to initiate her learners into this way of life that has in essence saved her own.

In the classroom, and in the coffee shop on 18th Street where we met, what Theresa cares about is the love of G*d that she has experienced and wants to share above all else. I do not use the word "mystic" or "mystical" lightly to portray Theresa and her teaching. Although I think the term can be overused, I have used it to title this portrait because I think it is appropriate. I use the descriptor with an understanding—one closer to what Theresa might suggest—that we are all called to be mystics.

The roots of the English word "mystic" include the Greek "*mystikos*," meaning an initiate—an initiate into a particular and secret way of life conscious of and affected by a direct and transformative presence of G*d. Christian mysticism represents the practices and beliefs associated with preparing for that religious experience.[4] This is precisely what Theresa had claimed she "was on fire for." Her unconventional ways are better brought under this descriptor because the term can contain what seems like the incongruent love of G*d and Tradition, and also oppositional critique of the institution. Theresa holds all of these with no feelings of inconsistency. This is the creative path Theresa described that both questions the institution and follows the G*d of her understanding. She admitted doing so is a "tightrope" for a person and as a teacher.

> Now do I believe Catholics are the best? Of course I do. . . . But, there are problems with the Church, obviously. I heard a quote from a bishop explaining why people are leaving the Episcopal Church. You could say the same about almost any church.
>
> The bishop took a moment, which seemed to be an inhalation and exhalation of despair at the reality: "I think we have failed. We have become an institution focused on our own survival, and when an institution of faith community focuses on survival, it loses its creativity. It loses its ability to risk. It tends to hunker down and focus on things that are most important to the people who are still in the institution itself, rather than the kind of expansiveness and openness to newness that institutions need to grow and thrive."

Theresa shared this recollection to explain what she thought was happening now. While the institutional church has lost its creativity and its true focus, there are those people who are "walking the tightrope" preserving

---

4. McGinn, *Essential Writings of Christian Mysticism*.

tradition and also remaining open to ongoing revelation. She again spoke to Jackie and me of "the absurd and diverse" saints that do so. While she always qualified that category by saying she was not a saint, I would argue that given they are her models, that this is where she has come to fit within tradition.

> I am very passionate but my husband would say, what's the word? It's a good word too. It's not disrespectful, but . . . irreverent. Yes. I am irreverent . . . you know, not afraid to say how it is—regardless of who is in the room . . . but I think I still fit. I think you can remain catholic and be irreverent . . . I think you can be irreverent within the system. In a sense, I think that's what a lot of the saints do. Not that I am anything like a saint. Within the con . . . —I hesitate to call them confines, but within the structure of the church— I definitely think there is a need and a place for someone who is irreverent. It keeps . . . [church leadership] on their toes.

Jackie, it could be argued, demonstrates a similar desire, hope, and faith in her struggle to find a place to fit within the Catholicism with which she both identifies and critiques. She learned and has chosen an active and creative path, but laments not having language yet to describe it adequately. The depth of her views and insistence on action lie at the root of the dissonance she feels with conventional Catholicism. She is a woman of religious action that she does not witness as always present in the institutional church. What she witnesses there is too often misogynistic, conservative, and hurtful. Jackie continues to be connected in thought and action to Catholic social justice groups. She is running the New York Marathon for Catholic Charities—but is not interested in institutional membership.

Jackie shared with me, and repeated in our final conversation, the difficulty she faces, and acknowledged that some women have been able to resolve the tension she feels.

> What I saw in my grandmother was that her religion was not just your personal belief in G*d. It was the way you served others. . . . It's funny because this is the same woman who was angry with her own children for waiting too long to baptize their children. There is a tension I get stuck on. My grandmother apparently was able to resolve the tension between the institution and her own Catholicism. While she followed almost all the rules, I feel like she was also someone who also didn't believe very much in the institution. . . . She spent a lot of time and a lot of effort on women's Catholic education. She helped found a Catholic high school. . . . She was really a church leader and a lot of her work focused on

women. Because of her I see that as part of being Catholic, so it's hard for me to find my place in it, and make sense of it.

At this point, our final conversation became even more interesting. Theresa and Jackie connected on their shared experience of the class where they taught and learned together. Jackie described how the class had upended her expectations. She remembered thinking, "How is she getting away with this?" The jolting revelations of social sin, injustices toward women, and the female heroism in the face of terrible consequences shook her loose of old views. Listening to Jackie's reflective responses to hers and my questions, as I had worried, Theresa did turn on her "teacher moves" and began campaigning for, or inviting, Jackie to return to the Church. Theresa admitted to her former student that the church has "failed absolutely in many ways" but that it is her prayer and hope for the future that feeds her faith. Theresa, in teacher mode, brought the social justice Jackie had obviously integrated back to G*d—particularly in and through the bodily and personal Jesus the Christ. This is from where she herself draws her view that all bodies are sacred. Theresa began sharing her story including much of what she had shared with me, up the point of her dark periods. Using euphemisms that made us all laugh, she side-stepped the darker details but invited Jackie to explore the intuitions and desires for prayer in her life. Theresa suggested to Jackie that what she was describing "might be G*d calling you back." But soon after she said this, Theresa recoiled. Theresa the teacher recoiled at the possible judgment she was leveling against her student who had just courageously shared her life and her views.

Theresa realized and articulated that what she was doing was "an advertisement." She recalled her own explicit description of her hopes and goals for her students to be reflective, more than anything else. In that personal practice is where Theresa believes G*d works. She suggested that it was when a person closes that door that a person might be lost. Theresa found it difficult to admit who and where Jackie was in her life reflected lostness at all. Realizing the dissonance between this position and her advertisement, Theresa demonstrated some embarrassment. She even emailed me afterward to describe a terrible nightmare she had concerning the judgment she feared she might have expressed. Theresa apologized profusely in the email and in our conversation.

In the context of our conversation, after catching what Theresa clearly felt had been an inappropriate judgment, she turned to me and asked what I was finding in my interviews, and what I hoped to write about. I shared that I wished to contribute to a larger more affirming conversation concerning questions like this and, at the very least, to engender a positive curiosity about the religious lives of young people like Jackie. The three of us noted that the current pope, or the Teacher of the Catholic Church, was currently encouraging dialogue beyond the old boundaries of tradition not unlike the one we were having. Theresa chuckled at the thought that she might have done something similar as a teacher. She commented that it sounded to her as if the new forms of religiousness I was investigating were like dark matter in deep space that is unrecognizable using standard measures because they can take so many forms, and that scientists theorize its existence because this matter in its many forms effect the matter around it in ways that can be observed. She expressed a warm and humble apology for possibly sounding like she judged Jackie or the idea that religiousness could be happening beyond affiliation. I do not think she had, but it clearly concerned Theresa that she had made the very mistake she had identified as her worst moment in teaching. Theresa requested more information on what I was reading and writing, and expressed the desire to learn more about what was happening in this area. While she did not verbalize that Jackie's religious education had been successful, she nodded in active and sincere listening as Jackie herself explained how it had been.

Theresa and Jackie, from their different levels of participation and affiliation, take seriously the contradictions and benefits of Catholic tradition. Neither possesses an absolute certainty about the authority of the church, but both are willing in their own ways to navigate the tensions, dilemmas, and conflicts that come with their Catholic inheritance. Theresa has found a way to do so on the inside, but far from any authority beyond her own relationship with G*d. Jackie does not believe she fits in any church that currently exists, but she does fit somewhere in the tradition that she learned from her family and this particular teacher. She is called to action because of it. Theresa's deeply spiritual and justice-seeking lessons, particularly surrounding women's rights, revealed the distance that often exists between the imperatives of Catholicism and the experiences of human persons. Theresa had presented "tradition at its best" and the reality that it often falls short. In the context of an all-girls high school, Theresa's teaching style and Jackie's experience reflect religious learning as a communal, reflective, and sacred activity.

In her book *Women's Way of Knowing*, Belenky and her colleagues argue that what they call "connected teaching" transforms the hierarchical separation of teacher and learner into a more symmetrical relationship.[5] Emma Percy suggests a similar goal using the image of mothering.[6] These authors suggest that when patriarchal models of knowledge and transmission are rejected, and space is provided for women to learn through different means, learning occurs through the claiming of one's own voice.[7]

Both Theresa and Jackie are products of this process. Walking the creative path of questioning institutional religion at the same time actively following the G*d of their understanding is indeed a tightrope as Theresa claimed. Winter et al. argue that women like Theresa and Jackie who are taking responsibility for their own religious lives are not putting ultimate trust in themselves over against institutional Catholicism. "On the contrary. In learning to trust and value themselves and to honor their own intuitive wisdom, they are putting their unconditional trust in G*d, however they know or name the One who is Ultimate Authority."[8]

After learning with an educator who facilitated the experience as such a sacred and collaborative process, Jackie learned to walk this tightrope as well, while also claiming her own voice. After speaking with and listening to how Jackie had integrated the educational experience, Theresa admitted that she did not know how to describe the teaching as "successful," but that she could not call it a failure either. Theresa added, "I don't know what Catholicism will become in the future."

---

5. See Tauber, *Open Minds, Devoted Hearts*, 119.
6. Percy, *Mothering as a Metaphor for Ministry*.
7. Tauber, *Open Minds, Devoted Hearts*, 119.
8. Winter et al., *Defecting in Place*, 195.

chapter 4

THE DISAFFILIATING TEACHER

The portraits in the previous chapters suggest to theologians and educators that our map or chart of the religious landscape may need to be rethought. Our understandings of religious life and learning could be updated according to the variety of voices of people like Eliot and Theresa found at the edge of affiliation, and Michael and Jackie who dwell in and move through the edge itself. The image of a liquid modernity offers theologians access to the reality that the map and taxonomy of affiliated and disaffiliated is inadequate.

Dragons and other fantastical creatures once occupied the margins of maps and sea charts. Monsters awaited anyone who crossed the edges of the known. For most but not all people those beasts were a powerful deterrent to further exploration. We know the world better because of those who transgressed those boundaries. These portraits provide a view from the edge where we used to believe dragons existed.

In this chapter, the two teachers portrayed are themselves conflicted by their own religious affiliation. Both occupy the same space at the edge of affiliation as the disaffiliated former students encountered in the previous chapters. The two educators were ultimately unwilling or unable to identify and meet with a former disaffiliated student. I have included their portrait because our conversations and their teaching revealed a pattern that had not surfaced so significantly in the pairings that focused on the conversation between an affiliated teacher and their disaffiliated former student. Unlike Eliot and Theresa, Maria and James may be affiliated in name only for the sake of their jobs in Roman Catholic secondary schools. More than being critical of the institution, these two teachers are seeking out and living religious alternatives in their personal lives. Maria and

James both empathize with the critique, disinterest, and departure of their disaffiliating students.

Although these two educators identify as affiliated Catholics, our conversations suggest significant adjustment of their own relationship with the church's institutional or conventional authority that has moved them as educators off the map and further out into liquid modernity. These personal religious experiences have and continue to influence their teaching practice. Considering these two teachers simply as affiliated ignores the reflective process and movement in their lives that may not have led to full disaffiliation yet, but does reflect the religious options, mobility, and remixing associated with that. Although Maria and James identify as Catholic, they no longer attend Mass and have an ambivalent view of the institutional Roman Catholic Church. While they teach Catholicism, they have personally chosen what is essential and nonessential from that tradition to practice in their own lives. While this portrait does not portray the impact of that process on a particular former student, it does explore how the experiences of these two teachers influence their teaching hopes, goals, and practice. I invite you to imagine the religious educational results.

AN INITIAL SKETCH

James is a young, educated social studies and religious studies teacher. He is pursuing a doctorate in education while teaching at a Catholic high school. He has been teaching for fifteen years in both public and Catholic schools. James is thin, and wears glasses. When I met him in a classroom at Fordham University, he wore a Gore-Tex coat and a fleece underlayer. He had taken off his tie and unbuttoned his shirt. James is active and he does not sit still long. Though he was tired, it was not the end of his teaching day. James had communicated over email that he would need to hurry on to a tutoring gig in a neighboring town immediately after our interview. He had asked for sample questions prior to our meeting and brought handwritten notes to the questions I provided. James was a little worried about his responses, but soon became more comfortable speaking spontaneously. He is passionate about meeting students where they are—which is very similar to where he is: They (and he) feel the church is out of touch with contemporary life.

Maria is a middle-aged Latina in her second career. She has also been teaching for fifteen years. Maria's posture in the classroom and at our initial interview communicated a no-nonsense demeanor. Her journey from

Madison Avenue to religious education follows a boomer generation seeker narrative after a series of disillusionments and tragedies. The institutional church has failed her, and she is in the process of creating a substitute for church on her own and with friends. Maria approaches teaching with a very broad definition of religion she learned in graduate school. She is not concerned with the affiliation of her students, but believes the boundaries of Christianity morality are helpful.

Both James and Maria were born and raised in New York City, and have been influenced by its culture and diversity. They described their families as culturally Catholic, but not practicing. Both educators shared stories of periods of active participation and affiliation in their lives, as well as the replacements they now practice in a period of much less participation. They described their current continued Catholic affiliation in cultural terms, and for professional reasons.

MEETING JAMES AND MARIA

When I met James for an initial conversation to explain the study and answer any questions he might have, he was eager to share his frustrations and concern that religious education and campus ministry were teaching and preaching from the "same binders full of yellowed and disintegrating paper they had had since the '70s." This theme of the church being out-of-date and out-of-touch became a refrain for James. I explained to James at our first meeting that this was an initial visit to invite him to participate in the study, but if he had time I would be happy to stay and talk. He signed the consent letter and away we went.

What struck me in speaking with James that day and in our following conversations were his compounding concerns that were echoed in the comments of his students. He mentioned one common nickname given to a certain type of religious educator and minister that worried him—"the Catholic Taliban." James seemed to be accustomed to this suggestive image of violent anachronism among his students. His commentary of concerns came freely and quickly, and he wondered aloud whether he should say it on tape. This initial conversation was not being recorded, but we were in his classroom with the door open. I reminded him that I would be recording our next interview, but that he could ask me to turn it off at any time, and that his identity would be kept confidential. I also stated that I was taking notes now. He acknowledged, and continued our conversation.

His mother and grandparents raised James after his father passed away when James was in the third grade. Many members of his family stopped going to church after his father died. James attended Catholic schools from pre-kindergarten through to college. In high school, he chose, on his own, to attend Mass and even teach CCD. James would go to Mass by himself for Christmas and Easter. "I have always had an interest in religion," he explained. "I didn't have the desire to go out. I don't drink or do drugs. I didn't do any of that in college either. I just had zero interest in it. I think there were worse things to do than to go to church by yourself." Then and now, James had a difficult time articulating his image of G*d. He distilled his theology into ideas of action, like loving others as oneself. This is what he has learned being Catholic means.

James volunteered as a catechist from high school through graduate school. He continued five years into his teaching career. He shared that while working at public schools, he attended Mass more often because it was something he intentionally sought out. James kept his volunteering a secret, however, because he finds those who aggrandize themselves by sharing the many good deeds they do "off putting." He explained, "Trying to do a tradition more often and better than somebody else is really missing the whole point, in my opinion." James noted that now he is working at a Catholic school he attends Mass much less, participating in community service projects every Saturday instead. James characterized the groups in which he participates as "genuine people coming together to do something genuine."

In what at first seemed like a non sequitur, James explained that he does not go out to the bars like others his age, and that he is the only one in his family that does not own a luxury car. To complete his thought, he explained: "I am looking for genuine connection. I think that that is what people who go to bars and talk about their BMWs are also looking for." James shared in our first conversation that this search has included participating in large evangelical megachurch events, attending synagogue with his Jewish girlfriend, and questioning the institution of the church. He noted how funny it has been teaching religion and hearing his students ask the same questions he began asking a decade earlier in his own life. Yet knowing how to respond to those questions in the role of a Catholic religious educator is a challenge for James.

Like meeting James, Maria surprised me with her responses. One might judge her as a member of the old guard when it comes to Catholicism. But doing so would be wrong. After first rocking back to chuckle and smile at my comment and question, she returned to make eye contact and explain her approach to teaching religion.

> Religion is something bigger than going to church. . . . Religiousness for me is not religious. [laughs] It's not religious in the traditional sense. You know, its loving life . . . being open to other people. For me it is just a way of being in the world.
>
> As a teacher, I am definitely not an evangelizer. I am not into that. . . . I teach religion, first and foremost, as an academic subject. For me, it's not about getting someone to believe in what I believe. It has been a journey of discovery for me to come to what I believe. . . . So, teaching religion is like teaching any other academic subject. . . . That is what is fun for me, . . . the learning and discovery. I'm also learning in the process of covering things that I hadn't come across before.

When I met Maria in a classroom at Fordham University, she shared an early religious memory. Maria attended Catholic schools as a child. What she learned there made her feel shameful about her family who did not attend church. Although her mother had religious statues, pictures, and altars at home, young Maria was worried that her mother was going to hell. So to help her mother get into heaven, she blessed her when her back was turned. Maria shared that the G*d she learned about in Catholic school was punishing. "I was afraid of G*d. Afraid of what would happen. . . . That G*d would orchestrate my mom going to hell because she didn't go to Mass." When she was in her late teens, Maria's father had a conversion experience and began attending Mass regularly. Her mom still would not go. She explained that her family never spoke of religion at home. There was just an understanding that they were Catholic.

"The Boundaries Are Boss": Tradition as Emphasized by Ecclesial Authorities

Both James and Maria are well-trained religious educators. James studied theology and history as an undergrad, and then earned a master's degree in curriculum. In our conversations, he noted the difference between teaching religion and teaching social studies. He described teaching religion as more dynamic than other subjects where he has a state curriculum to teach and standards are set. In his religious courses, he hopes to facilitate an experience that is more personal. But he admitted the challenge of having to teach the beliefs, practices, and tradition of the Catholic Church. "It's kind of like having a state curriculum." He both bemoaned and defended the mandated *Doctrinal Elements of a Curriculum Framework for the Development of Catechetical Materials for Young People of High School Age* implemented by the USCCB. "They say it's not a curriculum, it's a framework. *But it is a curriculum.* You can only choose from two textbooks."

Maria, who earned an MA and a PhD in religious education, likewise expressed the challenge she feels to breathe life into the narrow religious curriculum mandated by the USCCB. On the first page of the textbook she is required to use, before any of the content of the curriculum begins—or perhaps as its very first element—the authors and publisher quote respondents of recent studies in which young people resist the exclusivism of affiliation-based religion and criticize the institutional church. "They say religion has become associated with church attendance and commitment to orthodox beliefs," the book explains. "'Being spiritual but not religious' may also be associated with something else: egotism." The curriculum that these two, and all religious educators in Catholic schools in the United States, are required to use accuses disaffiliating Catholics of being "complacent and self-centered" because they are not held accountable in relationships and they do not serve the common good.

Despite or maybe because of such attitudes, Maria likes to "twist her students' lens on what it means to be religious." Through films, readings, reflections, and discussions that at first might not be recognized as religious, she reveals religious questions and themes concerning the "broad strokes of life" that the material explores. Maria operates with this expansive definition of religion in her academic approach because it includes the "spiritual" in the "spiritual but not religious." She essentially performs an end run around the concerns of the USCCB. She is not teaching her students to be spiritual. Her definition of religion is simply more spiritual. "I love it when kids write things like, 'I had no idea this film or book was "religious."' [laughs]. . . . Some students want to rebel against religion. They don't buy it. They don't understand me at first when I say this [course is] not about 'do you believe or do you not believe.' . . . Every now and then I open the door on that for the kid who is mature enough to understand it."

Maria shared a story that illustrates her approach to teaching religion, and contemporary context in which she does so. How she told the story also supplies commentary on her methodology and theology. One of her supervising administrators once observed her class. She gave a great class and the majority of his comments were positive. However, according to Maria, "he said, you never mentioned Jesus. You never said 'Jesus' the whole time." Maria bit her lip at that moment but shared her internal response with me: "And your point is? [laughs] It was like, I hadn't branded it!" This is a provocative but also significant story that illustrates a tension for a teacher like Maria today.

Maria explained that her supervisor's comment demonstrated a distinction she herself felt in her life, in the branding economy language with which she was familiar.[1] She had positively and effectively communicated religious meaning and tradition to students to which they could relate from their multiple and diverse points of entry. Despite the pluralism present in her classroom and the world, to Maria, what apparently mattered to the institution for which she worked was their "branded" way of relating to G*d. That was not what had moved her in her own religious journey of discovery. Maria experienced this view as a foreclosure compared to the theology she learned in her formal religious education. Mary's story suggests a stern warning that church leaders and educators should take seriously. Who is it that is being complacent and self-centered?

While Maria's determined teaching style does not include what she called "religious branding," her teaching does involve presenting a question and providing as much interesting and compelling information related to that question as she can. From there, she invites her students to share and reflect. Like all of the teachers portrayed here, Maria teaches with what Thomas Groome calls shared-praxis pedagogy. The methodology expands the epistemological base of religious education by rejecting deposit approaches to teaching religion. Rather than an indoctrinating delivery system, Groome's dialectical hermeneutic reframes teaching to invite learners to integrate an interpretation of the Christian tradition in such a way that they are equipped to respond to ever-new situations.[2] That broad definition of religiousness Maria teaches and the way she teaches it reflects her formal training, as well as her own individual search.

Maria's favorite topic to teach is other religious traditions. She felt she might convert to Judaism not long ago. Maria believes the world's religions are "different paths up the same mountain." And because her goal is to "open

---

1. Maria's first career was in media and advertising. Tom Beaudoin addresses the power of branding and its powerful connections to religion and spirituality. See Beaudoin, *Consuming Faith*.

2. Groome, *Christian Religious Education*.

The Disaffiliating Teacher

the door" on her students' narrow views of religion, she often explores the similarities and differences between the world's religions with her students. Doing so, Maria argued, can improve one's understanding and appreciation of one's current religious identity. James also enjoys teaching comparative religion. He created a world religions course and loves teaching it more than his other religious courses for similar reasons.

James confessed that as much as he chafes at the limits of the required curriculum, he sees the point of the framework's attempt to standardize religion classes. "They don't want students from every Catholic School coming out having different ideas of Catholicism, or not knowing much about Catholicism." That said, he returns quickly to his earlier critique. As a New Yorker, he does not give much credence to consensus. He is well acquainted with permanent cultural difference—especially within Catholicism. He shared that his own religion teachers were always the most "free spirited, almost hippie," of all his teachers. "They were the creatives. They stood out from the other subject teachers. That is the experience I come from. So, what I do is creative. It is not textbook or test driven." James often vacillated between these two positions—understanding the church's resistance to change and the critique of the Church being so out of touch. In the interview and in the classroom, he walks the tightrope Theresa described. James put it this way, "Sometimes the Bishop's framework is helpful for reminding me of content or concepts I don't remember from undergrad. But I have to update it, and tweak it, like Vatican III style."

Both James and Maria shared that affiliation with the Catholic Church is not their goal as teachers of religion. However, despite their struggle with the boundaries they are provided (because they are not their own), they recognize the institutional reason for them and choose to play their role. Maria sees the value of keeping students connected to Christian identity and morality because "so many boundaries have been lost." In a funny autocorrect in the interview transcript, this line was first recorded as "the boundaries are boss." I laughed, corrected it, and continued coding. The idea, however, kept showing up. These two educators struggled with the fact that they were *living* outside the boundary but were *employed* by those defining and holding the boundary itself. In a sense, the boundaries really are their boss.

James also spoke of this tension and added that he has shared his concerns with colleagues and was told to refer this students to the Vatican website or website of the United States Council of Catholic Bishops for more information when he is uncomfortable with student questions concerning church positions. Beyond this referral, he shared that one colleague advised him to tell his students, "The church will change when the Holy Spirit sees fit to guide it through that change." James quipped that while he understood his colleague's point, he could not teach that "with a straight face. That's BS. And they [his students] know it. They're teenagers." James explained that one of the things his students tell him that makes him effective as a religious educator is that he is not a "professional Christian." "Religion doesn't dominate my life. It is an element of my life amongst other elements." In this regard, James's teaching presents a strong implicit value of service, but not of affiliation. He identifies as Catholic, but restrains laughter at his student's critical comments of the church, one comment in particular:

> These students are savvy New Yorkers. They will say things that sound sarcastic but are poignant, theologically speaking. . . . The students laugh every time the textbook mentions Vatican II like it's this unbelievable moment. I try not to laugh as well, but I don't get it either. The textbook says VATICAN II!!! So the students are, OK. What is it? The book and I try to break it down as a watershed moment of change and update for the Church in 1965. The students just laugh. They say, "That is really sad that they are so proud that their last update was in 1965." We live in a world that changes rapidly. The fact that there are pages dedicated to a latest update in 1965 just reveals how out of touch from their lives the church is.

James teaches passionately about the challenges of being Christian in contemporary society because it is a tension he experiences. Finding time to be contemplative, being compassionate in New York City, forgiving those who trespass against you are not values or activities that are "advertised in any way, shape, or form," he explained. James described that what he enjoys about teaching religion is trying to connect church teachings and religious ideas to students' lives and interests. I observed his students take the major facts and figures of a saint's live and turn it into a social media campaign or website. Most of his students come from families in finance or business. His students quickly responded to the lesson James taught because it was done in and through an activity they understood. However, implicit in the successful educational activity was a compounding critique of the antiquated nature of the church. When students found their local parishes online, they commented on how out of date their websites were, and that they often had no social media presence.

What James enjoys about teaching religion is that some students may never have thought deeply about questions of life, meaning, morality, and death, and they may never again. James suggested, "This religion stuff, social justice and thinking of others, is a curve ball. I think they can be transformative . . . and greater than any textbook can teach." James clearly articulated the cross pressure he feels in contemporary culture and in his role as a Catholic religious educator. Despite the enjoyment he had just explained, he does not think it is appropriate to share his own views in class. When there is a question concerning the validity of a church teaching, James admitted often letting students sort out the answer or having to explain that "it's just what the Vatican says" before moving on. Like James, rather than affiliation, Maria articulated that she wants her students to walk away from her classes having learned that

> religion is simply the intuition that there is something larger, not a belief, but a knowing. . . . That is my theology of teaching. . . . We don't have all the answers. The way I am and the way I teach religion is not really, really religious in any traditional sense. It isn't you have to believe this, or you have to believe that, and you have to do this or that. I never speak in those terms.

James shared that the more some of his students learn about the church through the provided Bishop's Framework, the more they realize it should not be a big part of their lives. The church is "out of touch and does not offer them anything." He added, however, an interesting distinction that his students make, and one that mirrors his own experiences. "They'll say they had a great experiences with high school religious studies classes, doing service learning and immersion trips, but they will connect that with the school, not with the church. They explain the school is doing a great job presenting the Catholic faith, but when they go out there I hear a lot of alumni say it's a different dynamic in parishes." James admitted he understands why so many students do not want to be a member of something so conservative and institutional. While he does not attend Catholic Mass often, James noted that other religious teachers from different traditions were communicating better with people in the twenty-first century.

OUT ON WATERS—PORTRAITS FROM THE EDGE OF AFFILIATION

FINAL PORTRAIT: HOW THE BOUNDARIES WERE LOST

My conversations with Maria and James worked backward from their challenging experiences teaching religion today into their own life stories and significant religious learning that brought them to their current ambiguous affiliation. Their life histories added dimension and texture to the complicated relationship they have with religious authority and institution today, and how it influences their teaching. James told me a story about a class he took while working on his MA in which the instructor asked the typical question you first ask a group of student teachers, "Why did you become a teacher?"

> I became a religious educator because [religion] was very formative for me growing up. . . . When I was in the third grade, my father passed away. I remember every single teacher coming to the wake. . . . I thought the wake is for the immediate family. . . . But every single teacher from the school came. The school was K–8 so most of the teachers I didn't know. All the nuns and priests came too. I learned I was a part of something. School took on a bigger meaning for me than just getting a good grade. . . . I realized this was a community that cares. This is a community that comes together. I thought it was a very genuine Christian thing to do. . . . That impacted me. I wanted to be a teacher because I thought it was about helping someone beyond the classroom.

Maria also began her path teaching religion for a distinct reason, but one that started much later in life. Besides attending Catholic high school, Maria had little sense or connection with the church. After high school, she wanted to live independently like Mary Tyler Moore and other TV personalities. She went into business, lived in an apartment with her sister in Manhattan. "Church? Religion? They had nothing to do with me at all. I wasn't opposed. I wasn't rebelling. It just wasn't part of the equation." Maria became a religious educator through what she called a "journey of discovery" that included both success and loss.

Maria had broken through the glass ceiling in a large media company when she found herself in the crossfire between two bosses. She unfortunately learned how "evil people are, not can be, are." She described one particularly terrible day:

> As I was walking out the revolving door in the lobby, I thought, "the devil does exist." And that was the beginning. The beginning

> of my conversion. It was the first time I had thought about G*d in I don't know how long. . . . That was my feeling. The devil does exist. And I felt this pull to run to a church to exorcise it from me.

When I asked her what came next, she replied, "I started going to church, a lot."

Maria described this turning point as a moment of conversion. She used that term and the expression, "a tap on the shoulder" to describe what called her back. She told a delightful story of finding the church on her block that she had never noticed but then could not walk past without stopping in. "Any time I saw lights on . . . I wasn't just going to pray. I went to find out what was going on . . . I got involved. . . . It became my second home." She felt that it was her church. But even then, Maria did not attend Mass often. From this first discovery, Maria began to inquire more about religion in general and realized she loved studying the subject. It was a four- or five-year process in conversation with her pastor and others before she realized that her interest and enjoyment of studying religion were not going away.

In her late forties, Maria began taking graduate courses in religion and religious education. She continued working in business but was not happy there. Maria had not planned on making a career change, but she was disillusioned with the corporate world and knew she would need to make a decision. She loved what she was learning.

> As I was finishing my MA, I knew I was going to go on for a doctorate. I just knew I wasn't going to stop. . . . It was just fun. It was all so interesting. . . . The first class I took mentioned that 80 to 90 percent of people in the pews have only a third grade level understanding of religion. That blew my mind because I had been afraid all that time that I would be found out. But then the professor was telling us that everyone else didn't know either.

Maria recounted how her professors "opened the door wide"—both opening *a way into* seeing religion in a more expansive way, and opening *a way out of* the limitations of how religion had been presented to her as both child and as an adult. One professor in particular impressed upon Maria an expansive definition of religion. "So I left behind the old narrow ideas." While her religious education courses expanded her views of religion, she explained it also led to another disillusionment. Maria shared that she had interpreted her discovery and enjoyment in her studies as a sign or call to pursue religion personally and professionally: "But I think I interpreted incorrectly."

Then, during her studies, the diocese closed Maria's church.

What Maria described as a growing, vibrant, community, and her home for twenty years was suddenly shuttered, splintered, and gone. Like her experience in the corporate world, it was another blow to where she thought she would fit. She added that her church closing was not her first experience with this aspect of institutional church. Another parish where she had developed a network of friends had shut down two years before that. Maria felt empty and angry. She has found a new parish but shared she does not want to be there. "I don't want to go.... I have felt no guilt about just not going on Sundays.... It is ok that I am not going to Mass.... I am replacing Mass with a personal retreat to a different type of home." Maria spends her Sunday mornings at a beautiful park reading and writing. It is where she wrote most of her dissertation and it has become one substitute for church. She is also co-creating another ersatz church-activity with a group of her friends from her old church. They get together on a Friday or Saturday when they can match schedules. They call it movie night.

Both James and Maria have arrived in a similar place. They are disillusioned with institutional church, but not with the religion that transformed their lives at some point in their history. They were moved by religion and Catholic tradition, but have also been moved by disheartening experiences with how it is articulated by conventional authorities. Like the former students presented in the previous portraits, they have selected what is essential and not essential in tradition itself as they move on, but do not lose their sense of tradition. For these two teachers, attending church is not one of those essential pieces, nor is really believing what the institution teaches. They have replaced conventional practices and beliefs with a remix of their own reflective actions and view their choices and explanations as coherent, even if others might not. James and Maria both viewed their own religious educations as successful, despite their current dilemmas. Moreover, they believed their current teaching practice benefits their students.

James shared that his religious educational goal is to present religion as positively as possible. "I think people remember how they were treated and their experience in a class more than the content, or what was written in a book." He hopes his students have an experience where they may want to learn about religion again some time in their life. Maria's goal is to correct the bad theology with which her students come to her. She shared one such example she experienced herself after taking a class on ecumenism. Maria loved meeting and working with the various traditions of Christians and shared with the instructor her interest in the similarities they all shared. She characterized his response as a "real spoiler." He taught her, and the class, that the point of ecumenism is to bring them all back to the true church. "I thought, Wow. So I totally relate to the kids. There are just too many public disappointments with the church."

When I asked James if he still identified as Catholic after his own listing of disappointments, he replied that while he cannot erase his Catholic upbringing and education, he struggles with the institutional church.

> I was told to teach it's not the Church's job to . . . keep up with whatever fad is happening. But these aren't fads! These are women having the right to vote and Black-civil-rights-like change. . . . But I can't say that because I am being paid by the Catholic institution.

Though Maria shared a similar struggle, she is hopeful—but not in the Church as it is now. She believes that things have a tendency to return full circle. "We are going back to the way the church originally was. Very grassroots. Very welcoming. Very intimate. Like a meal among friends." Maria said she does not miss going to church. She misses her old community, but without that she does not think the church has anything to offer her.

These educators are teaching Catholicism or handing on tradition from an altered or broader understanding of religiousness or Catholicity than one based on adherence or affiliation. These portraits suggest contemporary religious educators can occupy the same fluid space as their students, and are open to ongoing conversion—and deconversion.

The Edge That Is a Place

chapter 5

DECONVERSION AND A DURABLE GOOD

In 1977, NASA's *Voyager* probes left earth to explore the known universe, expected to become the first human-made object to leave the solar system. However, NASA's assumptions about the boundary between known and unknown space were incorrect. When *Voyager 1* reached the edge of the heliosphere—the realm of the sun's gravitational influence—it did not pass into the nothingness of deep space. Moving at thirty-eight thousand miles per hour, *Voyager 1* traveled through this "edge" for eight years. What was supposed to be a clear boundary separating something from nothing, researchers then realized is a place.

On August 25, 2012, *Voyager 1* finally moved beyond "dipping its toes into interstellar waters" and left behind the bubble of the sun's influence to "set sail on the cosmic seas between the stars."[1] What intrigues scientists about these interstellar seas just beyond the sun's influence is how particle waves move around the sun's influence the way water flows around a rock.[2]

Not unlike this boundary, the edge of recognizable religious communities has grown wider thanks to the voyager-like research of scholars such as Tom Beaudoin and Elizabeth Drescher. This growing body of literature from the edge describes a fluid space where people can move into, around, and across once-consequential boundaries in order to believe and practice "otherwise."[3] Like those portrayed in this book, these individuals and groups have not given up religious beliefs or practices. Many of these so-called "Nones" are "non-practicing" Catholics like Jackie and Michael.

1. Fazekas, "Voyager at the Edge"; Landau, "NASA Confirms Voyager 1."
2. Landau, "NASA Confirms Voyager 1."
3. Taylor, *Secular Age*, 257.

A little more than half of all Catholics leave the church at some point in their lives.[4] As we have seen in the portraits, their stories are more complex than the common narrative of loss admits, and often more positive than a narrative of deficiency dares to realize. To tell the story of these "Lapsed" Catholics living and learning religiously in this edge that is a place means encountering them, not just counting them. The religious lives of this significant and growing group challenge our conventional expectations of religious identity and community because they similarly move around the Church's influence like water around a rock.

TEACHING WHO WE ARE AND HOW WE LEARNED TO LIVE THAT WAY

If it is true that "we teach who we are," this presents theologians and religious educators with interesting questions: Who are we in today's context characterized by so much choice, mobility, and mixing? How is liquid modernity influencing the religious life and learning of both contemporary learners and the educators teaching them religion? Could something good be happening here?

This chapter addresses these provocative questions and the related challenge that conventional paradigms of religious participation are inadequate to understand the portrayed teachers and learners. The presented portraits suggest that it is possible both to teach a sense of tradition and to allow learners to release that tradition onto new situations beyond the immediate influence of conventional religious affiliation. These educators have shifted their pedagogical and theological goals to reflect their own formative and religious educational experiences and to respond to the fluid world in which they and their learners live. Their disaffiliating learners have integrated into their lives the praxis-over-propositional approach to being religious that their teachers model.

Yet our present discourse of loss and our theology of affiliation prevent us from developing more affirming theological language that might help the persons portrayed here (and the many others like them) speak and be heard. Perhaps those portraits can help us to see with different eyes our "liquid modernity" and its varied options for religious life and learning.

The portraits suggest that the teaching styles and practical theologies of Theresa, Eliot, Maria, and James derive from personal experience and

4. Masci and Lipka, "Americans May Be Getting Less Religious."

reflection on their own evolving relationships. The practical interventions they make in their teaching reflect personal experiences over the course of their own lives. They are teaching who they are, and how they became who they are in a context characterized by choice, mobility, and remixing. They are modeling tradition. However, how that tradition is defined by conventional authorities is not the primary source or norm for their theologies or their religious educational practice. Their teaching draws from, and is an expression of, personal and practical theologies intimately involved with what they believe matters most. This is what they hand on.

Eliot's man cave montage with the maxim to "find G*d in all these things" is a lovely example of this approach to teaching and a significant element of the underlying theology that funds the teaching practice and faith of these educators: The Divine comes to us while participating in all of life. Praxis, then, represents the primary source for even the more systematic aspects of each of the teachers' theologies and pedagogies. For Theresa and Eliot, Maria and James exploring the significant educational influences that formed them and the revelation that shape their theology included identifying that some of those experiences that have outpaced doctrinal or ecclesial boundaries. Through a self-reflective exchange between primary and secondary theology, Eliot, Theresa, James, and Maria have transformed some Catholic practices. Affiliation is part of their identity in some way, but not the most significant part. Each of these educators believes and teaches toward a religious transformation or development they themselves experienced. They, in turn, model this praxis for their students.

Eliot, Theresa, Maria, and James were formed early in cultural circumstances where religious values and authority were givens. However, they each shared formative experiences and religious education that moved them out from this more static or "taken-for-granted-ness" of religious authority, religious belonging, and religious practice. By teaching who they have become in and through that process, and who they are continuing to become as they live and move in liquid modernity engaging with their students, they model and emphasize an active and ongoing process much less connected to denominational loyalty.

Both the religious educators and their disaffiliating students are the products of practical religious knowledge learned and developed through both formative personal experiences *and* formal religious education.

Religious life and learning for Eliot, Theresa, James, and Maria has been, and continues to be a process of faithful but critical reflection, and prayer. In their teaching, they invite their learners to develop a similar *phronesis* through ongoing *praxis* situated in their own everyday lives.[5] This active and relational way of being religious, and being Catholic, blurs hard edges of classification between affiliated and disaffiliating, religious and nonreligious, practicing and non-practicing Catholics.

LIVING AND TEACHING RELIGION WITH A "LIGHT TOUCH"

The praxis-over-propositional approach these teachers model is a profoundly imaginative and theological act. To perceive or experience G*d in All Things, as Eliot and his classroom teach, requires training learners not just in theological systems but in forming a religious imagination—which in turn influences the perceptions of self, the perceptions and relationship with the Divine, and the perceptions and hope of religious life. The latter includes living the tradition in innovative and less-affiliated ways. Michael articulated that one of the reasons he experienced Eliot as such an effective teacher was that he taught religion with this approach—what he called a "light touch."

Michael did not mean that Eliot's teaching was superficial. Precisely the opposite! What Michael meant by "light touch" was that Eliot's teaching practices were not doctrine heavy or overly affiliation based. Eliot and the other educators portrayed emphasized developing a more primary and practical ability to do theology themselves.

Jackie mentioned the same light touch and influential effect when she described Theresa's class with astonishment: "It was like she disguised a religion class as a women's studies course." Maria also offered a significant example of her "light-touch" approach when she admitted her definition of religion was "simply an introduction to living in relation to something larger." Moreover, she eschewed the idea of "branding" her religious studies class as Catholic. Even Theresa, whose Catholic-centric responses suggested at first that her approach was affiliation focused, soon revealed her more urgently expressed hope to develop in her students a habit of theological reflection that might lead to a spiritual awakening, as it did in her life.

For Theresa, as shown in her penny project, her fundamental concern was to awaken the inner voice and imagination of her students, and allow space for the Divine to "reach down" and communicate to the learner in

---

5. Miller-McLemore, *Wiley Blackwell Companion to Practical Theology*, 2.

a way only that person would understand. Theresa shared that in order to be able to teach in this way, the most important lesson she needed to learn was to suspend imposing her judgment and learn from her students. This highlights the shift from teaching doctrinal conclusions or propositions to teaching students how to do theology themselves. Though handing the task of theological reflection over to learners themselves is in fact quite "heavy," this is the light touch Michael and Jackie found so influential and that continues to organize their religious lives.

This imaginative response-ability and resulting relationship with the Divine was developed together with a teacher through the modeling and guidance experienced in religious education. Though Theresa hoped her students remain or become Catholic, the religiousness she cares about is a person's relationship with the Divine and their fellow human beings. While earlier cultural circumstances would have led students taught by teachers with approaches like Theresa's to become members of religious communities, the increased options and mobility of liquid modernity offers learners like Jackie and Michael who have integrated this praxis-over-propositional approach other viable religious options. I observed Theresa encounter this reality in a moving way during the final conversation with her former student, Jackie.

In the final interview, Theresa had begun to build up the Spirited momentum that both she and Jackie had described as part of her teaching style. Theresa was campaigning to show Jackie that the Catholicness she was hesitant to let go might be reason for her to return to the Church . . . but then she stopped. Theresa had just listened to her former student share her story and leapt into a lesson, a lesson that she realized might already have been learned. Theresa herself felt a dissonance and confessed that what she was doing felt like an "advertisement" (for the Church) rather than education.

As an educator, Theresa knew that any practice, text, or teaching that deepened or enriched a person's capacity for loving G*d and serving others was suitable material for religious study. Her gift as a teacher was to "disguise religion courses as a women's studies classes" and to confidently draw together seemingly disparate experiences to reveal their religious implications, and listen without judgment to the lives of her students. Like Eliot, Theresa showed her students how to find patterns of meaning in experiences, insights, and feelings from everyday life. In other words, she modeled the imaginative practice of finding G*d in All (these) Things.

Out of a profound faith and desire to value the young women in her classes, her light touch also includes her audacious way of transforming her teacher-learner relationships into more co-learning relationships that embodies what Sarah Taber calls "connected teaching."[6] She does this by relating to her students with a radical lack of self-concern, a desire to share the love of G*d, and a desire never to judge the voice of a student as less than her own. We can see from the lives of Michael and Jackie that such a "light touch" has enabled and encouraged ongoing religious imagination and reflection.

Rather than re-prescribing Christian norms, Theresa and Eliot engage their students by modeling openness, humility, and discernment. Michael pointed to this detail to explain what made his religious education most effective. His teachers shared honestly that being religious is an ongoing process. That prepared Michael not to expect that being religious was going to be one thing for the rest of his life.

These educator and learner portraits have shown that teaching religion with a light touch is about learning how to read one's personal experiences back onto tradition in a way that encourages the individual to become a very local, very personal theologian, extending tradition to new possibilities.[7]

CONVENTION VS. A SENSE OF TRADITION

David Hansen argues that the kind of changes that liquid modernity presents prompt two opposing reactions in institutional communities: the first views these changes as threatening and attempts to resist, the other recognizes that tradition can be handed on only as it takes on new modes of expression in and through encounters with difference in the world. Hansen uses the language of "traditionalism" vs. a "sense of tradition" to describe the distinction or dissonance my research participants experienced.[8] Like solids, traditionalism resists time, change, and fluidity. It attempts to be like rock and remain, as Pelikan famously described, the "dead faith of the living."[9] In contrast, persons and groups with a vital sense of tradition, especially in education, "can sustain a deep sense of cultural reverence

---

6. Tauber, *Open Minds, Devoted Hearts*, 119.
7. Beaudoin, *Witness to Dispossession*, 75.
8. Hansen, "Cosmopolitanism as Education."
9. Pelikan, *Vindication of Tradition*.

even while the actual objects of reverence may transform."[10] This sense of tradition is both much more fluid and, ironically, more durable because it is developed in dialogue.

In place of Hansen's language, I have chosen to use the framework of convention vs. tradition. The terms "conventional" and "traditional" represent the lived-in language that research participants used in our conversations to articulate this felt dissonance between the tradition they learned and the conventional religion they witness in the church as it is. For Jackie and Michael, this distinction of convention vs. tradition became more pronounced in and through their effective religious education.

Due to their experiences of this tradition in religious education and counterpoint experiences of conventional authority witnessed in the experienced authority of offensive homilies or "Paul Ryan Catholicism," Jackie and Michael felt a disorienting and disagreeable dissonance. As a result, they have both developed a critical resistance to convention, but also a constructive continuity with the sense of tradition they learned from their teachers. So doing, these two disaffiliating Catholics occupy an expanding religious space at the edge of affiliation with the church—where their teachers also live and move.

James shared that his former students often describe this dissonance between the religion they learned in school and the religion they witness in parishes. They (like James) connect with the sense of tradition they were taught in his classes, service trips, and retreats but not with the Catholic Church as it is the world. His perspective that the church is out of date resonates with Jackie's statement that she does not think a Catholic church exists where she would fit.

For James, Jackie, Michael, and Maria it was their religious educators who opened the door to this perspective and experience, and who "breathed new life into" their sense of being Catholic, their sense of being religious. However, faced with the "church as it is," Jackie and Michael as well as James and Maria felt they had no choice but to leave in order to continue to develop religiously. But note the effort Jackie and Michael, James and Maria have made in their lives and in our conversations both to resist and to situate themselves in continuity with the tradition that continues to organize and give meaning to their lives. Byron and Zeck's "exit interview" study of "lapsed" Catholics in Trenton, New Jersey, echoes the stories of Michael and Jackie, James and Maria as it reports many disaffiliating

---

10. Hansen, "Cosmopolitanism as Education."

Catholics do not believe that they are abandoning tradition but that the institution has abandoned them.[11]

Thus, Jackie does not describe herself as a "Lapsed Catholic." Instead, Jackie described thoughtfully how she learned and decided what type of Catholic she is, and would be. She lives an active sense of the tradition that continues to "hold her life together."[12] Jackie identifies with Catholic practices of justice and service. However, she is hesitant to use the title "Catholic" to describe her religious identity because of the conventional Catholicism she witnesses in moralizing "Paul Ryan and Pope Benedict Catholicism."[13] Jackie has experienced a very personal and real distinction between this conventional Catholicism she does not support and the tradition she was taught by her grandmother and Theresa. The tension that creates is exaggerated for Jackie because she learned this sense of tradition from two Catholic women,[14] but does not want to be associated with a church where she and these women are not able to participate equally.

Jackie and Maria most explicitly repudiated this aspect of the conventional Church. For Maria, her experiences of the institutional church mirrored a disillusionment and sexism she experienced in the corporate world and taught her the existence of evil. She had broken the glass ceiling only to be targeted by her male supervisors. In her new parish, after her home church had closed, the male pastor "tolerated" her women's groups but allowed them no real leadership, and at times seemed actively to undermine them. Moreover, among the most important theological corrections she must make in her teaching of young Catholic boys she listed the conventional Catholic view that "women are evil."

Maria and James present an interesting case study as affiliated but disaffiliating Catholic educators who are looking for the deeper aspects of their tradition that are often obscured by conventional and institutional

---

11. Byron and Zech, "On Their Way Out."

12. Tom Beaudoin offers this helpful working definition of what happens at the intersection of cultural and spiritual practice. See Beaudoin, "Secular Catholicism and Practical Theology."

13. Many studies have noted the connection between the disaffiliation of young adults from religious institutions and the politicization of religion by the Christian right, both Protestant and Catholic. Most recently see Spadaro and Figueroa "Evangelical Fundamentalism and Catholic Integralism."

14. Winter, Lummis, and Stokes describe the experience of many women in Christian churches who reject the patriarchy but participate on their own terms. They are, in their words, "defecting in place." See Winter et al., *Defecting in Place*.

sins. Like Jackie and Michael, it was Maria's formal religious education in graduate school that amplified her disillusionment with conventional Catholicism. It is working for a Catholic school that has made James aware of how out of touch the church is. He is searching out other religious and spiritual options.

Out of intuition, natural desire for growth, and the influence of religious education, these teachers and learners seek places beyond conventional expectations of orthodoxy where they are able to ask questions that matter, and find relationships that encourage them to be their authentic selves. Michael went to the Holy Land. Jackie taught writing in prisons. Maria got a PhD. James listens to Joel Osteen and attends his girlfriend's synagogue. In their religious education, these disaffiliating Catholics experienced a teaching-learning relationship where they were guided to grapple with challenging questions of life and religion, "out loud, with others."[15] In so doing, they were shown a tradition and were trained in its practices of theological reflection and active service, not a "branded" religious proposition.

As disaffiliating learners, Jackie and Michael are interesting cases in that they both have integrated such core elements of Catholic tradition: *Diakonia* and *Leitourgia*. For Jackie, it was the justice-oriented actions on behalf of the marginalized, especially on behalf of women, that continue to shape her life. Although it is not her explicit focus, she admits there is an inherent spirituality to such practice. Michael learned and loves the very Catholic perspective that the summit of *Leitourgia* is the Eucharist. Michael, when he does attend Mass, goes to experience the mystagogy and primary theology taught in and through the Lord's Supper. He is not coming with expectations of entertainment from the homily, but regularly leaves so frustrated by its content that he has begun developing his own liturgy with his fiancée on Sunday evenings and in his garden.

Michael consistently expressed the tension he feels between his learned sense of Catholic tradition and the exclusive self-authorizing tendencies of the institution he witnesses in the world. The theology he learned is more expansive than what he sees in local churches. Both Michael and Jackie's innovated practices and critical sense of tradition reflect that they have learned broader and more fluid theologies, are committed to ongoing learning, and are open to new ways of expressing themselves and their faith. This ability to do theology themselves, and their related choice of departure,

---

15. Syverson, "30 Million American Christians."

was catalyzed by exposure to diverse points of view and practical religious knowledge modeled for them in formal religious education. This reaction might have occurred with or without the presence of religious education. The introduction of this catalyst, however, reduced the energy needed and increased the possibility of a transformation by encouraging encounters and enabling mixing.[16] In other words, their religious educators helped facilitate an inevitable and natural process. The following sections offer a theoretical analysis of that natural process.

LEARNING IN THE PRESENCE OF DIFFERENCE

In the lives of both the learners and educators portrayed here, the experience of diversity and religious difference formed and continues to inform who they are, what they teach, and how they practice their sense of tradition. Their experience of how conventional authorities react to difference, whether it be gender or pluralism, often falls short of the tradition they have learned and integrated. They therefore teach and prefer to learn Catholicism with a lighter touch, a touch that flows around institutional forms that resist finding G*d in all these things.

Individuals and small groups living and learning religiously in response to their everyday lives and relationships drive theological development. The religious systems within which people live, move, and construct their meaning develop and change over time, just as individuals ideally do. Robert Kegan characterizes the new sociocultural demands in each new age as educational curriculum that teaches more appropriate, or contemporary, maturity. As in the story of the Sion Sisters (chapter 2) who contended with conventional anti-Semitism in light of their own encounters with Jewish neighbors, Kegan argues that the greatest catalyst of this epistemic growth is the experience of difference that presents new views that cannot be accommodated without changing one's meaning frame.[17]

Mary C. Boys agrees that learning in the presence of difference—religious difference in particular—represents a significant religious educational gift of liquid modernity to both individuals and religious traditions.[18] She argues that religious education done in the reality of religious pluralism engenders embarrassment at attempts of absolutism and

---

16. Helmenstine, "What Does a Catalyst Do?"
17. Kegan, *In Over Our Heads*, 210.
18. Boys and Lee, *Christians & Jews in Dialogue*.

provides learners tools for responding to this wider world.[19] The portraits of this study reveal this effect. Jackie, for example, hesitates to use the term Catholic to describe herself due to its historical and contemporary injustices. Similarly, after his experiences in Palestine/Israel and in his diverse neighborhood, Michael feels that the exclusive boxes of this religion vs. that religion obscure the sacred for the sake of self-interested concerns. Boys echoes these voices and suggests that conventional rendering of religion often fails to foster healthy human or Christian development by creating and sustaining partisan identities.[20]

Eliot, Theresa, Maria, and James are also suspicious of the way a more conventional Catholicism speaks of others who do not share the same story.[21] Maria shared a disheartening experience of attending an ecumenical conference with her pastor. This priest countered her excitement over the conversations happening at the conference by explaining that the real reason for ecumenical dialogue was to convert others to Catholicism. Eliot likewise confessed that he might have more in common with a disaffiliating person that an affiliated Catholic who was affiliated for the wrong reasons.

A significant part of the teaching objectives and practices shared by the educators encountered here set out to breathe life into a dying traditionalism and update the mandated lifeless curriculum. To use James's words, based on their own experiences learning in the presence of more than one religious account of reality, these educators update the tradition, "Vatican III style." Educators like Eliot, James, Maria, and Theresa foster dialogue with difference and its developmentally appropriate deconstruction of exclusivist religious teachings.

The portraits show a pedagogically persistent religious praxis and a mature religiousness that has relativized religious authority and resituated the locus of that authority from external conventional sources to lived experience in dialogue with a developed sense of tradition. From Kegan's perspective, such deconstruction and reconstruction that occurs in and through encounters with pluralism involve an epistemic change in subject-object relations. This change is required if people today are to develop the higher order of consciousness that is required for making sense of the demands of contemporary life.[22]

19. Boys, *Has God Only One Blessing?*, 27.
20. Boys, *Has God Only One Blessing?*, 9.
21. Boys, *Has God Only One Blessing?*, 30.
22. Kegan, *In Over Our Heads*, 34.

Kegan's model theorizes that what a learner is "subject to" has been "written on them" by an external authority. Despite its external origin, early in development a person identifies completely with these conventions.[23] Michael, for example, knew he was Catholic as a child because of the side of the aisle his family sat on in his childhood ethnic parish. For Michael and Jackie, religious education helped catalyze a movement of more and more knowledge to an "object" relation—where a person can hold it at arm's length, look at, investigate, take responsibility for, deconstruct, and integrate it with other ways of knowing.[24] Subject-object theory and religious education suggest a developmental quality to this moving out from taken-for-granted-ness that teaches openness to the challenge presented by religious pluralism[25]—but also a religious dimension.

DECONSTRUCTION ON BEHALF OF THE UNEXPECTED

When Theresa explained her desire to shock her students into listening for more than what they expected in her classes, she articulated an essential element of teaching theology well: to provoke conversations that would "open doors and windows to let new thoughts come in." John Caputo argues that the practice of deconstruction of conventional religious teachings and institutions on behalf of new experiences represents a posture and activity inspired by the Divine, that can even be a form of prayer.[26]

We see this idea that deconstruction is vital but not an end in itself in the lives of Jackie and Michael. The faithful but critical deconstruction they learned reveals points of tension in conventional expectations and unmasks institutional failures. Jackie was explicit that "there was not a Catholic Church that exists where she would fit." She serves her community as a teacher and political activist. Michael loves the liturgy but is so regularly disappointed by its leadership that he is finding his own way to deepen his relationships. The goals of their practices are the pursuit of justice and a closer relationship with the Divine—and that invariably involves reconstructing meaning as well.[27]

23. Kegan, *In Over Our Heads*, 34.
24. Kegan, *In Over Our Heads*, 34.
25. See Boys, *Has God Only One Blessing?*, 22.
26. Caputo, *What Would Jesus Deconstruct?*, 55.
27. Derrida and Caputo, *Deconstruction in a Nutshell*.

Deconversion and a Durable Good

For Jackie and Michael who learned, and still love, their sense of Catholic tradition, that sense promises something not realized in the church "as it is." Likewise, Caputo argues it would be idolatrous to identify the promise of religion provisionally housed in what he calls the "name" of religion and with the present state of affairs, and defend it as such.[28] Jackie and Michael learned this in large part from their religious educators in their praxis-over-propositional approach to teaching religion. The teachers shared the significant and formative experiences that catalyzed a deconstruction and transformation of their own religious lives and learning on behalf of the promise of their faith. Theresa, Eliot, James, and Maria learned in their own lives to deconstruct the image of the church as a perfect sacrament in order to come to their present realistic view of the church as it is. The educators spoke of the role of the Spirit in this maturing process. Eliot even expressed an affirming hope that what comes out the other end of this cultural period and developmental process might "be more Christian" than what exists now.

There is an important educational and religious dimension to this hope and the horizon it implies. Its theological significance lies in its response to the promise and what Derrida calls the absolute future that takes us by surprise. Caputo explains, "G*d is the possibility of the impossible, the wholly other, the unforeseeable, the one who breaks down our ego-logical and mono-logical preoccupation and exposes us to the coming of the other, the incoming of what we did not see coming" (asterisk added).[29] Eliot puts this theology into religious educational practice and into very concise words: "When in doubt, I lean toward being open. Absolutely."

The portraits of these religious teachers and learners in conversation suggest that the learned habit of deconstruction on behalf of the intuited or experienced promise provisionally housed in conventional forms is more than mere criticism. Otherwise it would not retain such a meaningful practice in the lives of Michael and Jackie. The religiousness that remains is experiential and draws upon those experiences and relationships that invite, call, or reveal what is "living and stirring" in tradition in order to "release it, set it free, and give it a new life."[30] The religious pedagogies articulated by the educators portrayed could best be described as deconstructive in this receptive and expansive sense.

---

28. Caputo, *What Would Jesus Deconstruct?*, 59.
29. Caputo, *What Would Jesus Deconstruct?*, 55.
30. Caputo, *What Would Jesus Deconstruct?*, 68.

Theresa, Eliot, James, and Maria are open to the coming of the unexpected, and are open to the lives of their students. Why? It is how the Divine has acted in their lives, and how they have come to the practical religious knowledge they feel compelled to hand on.

Sharing a faithful but critical praxis and releasing that sense of tradition out onto new situations are not mutually exclusive. This traditioning process enlarges and clarifies tradition itself. However, church history demonstrates the contested conversations involved with that process. Deconstruction as an essential element of religious life and learning is indeed a risky idea if one is invested in keeping the boundaries of the church as it is. As Caputo says, it is dangerous because it threatens the "pretense of the present form of things."[31] This conversion through deconstruction initiates a process that can lead a learner outside of the boundaries associated with conventional religion, and challenges the theology of affiliation as being the only faithful option. It is risky, but the portraits suggest that the faithful but critical praxis of deconstructing conventional forms reflects important developmental steps that individuals and the tradition require.

DECONVERSION AS RELIGIOUS DEVELOPMENT

The portraits suggest developmental, educational, and theological reasons to recognize deconversion as a successful outcome of religious education, and an ongoing form of religious life and learning. Barbour and Streib use the term to designate a positive process of learned mobility and legitimate transformation that occurs during the search for an adequate system of beliefs and practices.[32] Maria Harris argues that such critical deconstructive questioning is the "center of the teaching act," for it compels learners to reach from lower stages of consciousness toward more complex and appropriate ways of knowing.[33] According to Kegan, these more appropriate ways of knowing involve the capacity both to author one's own perspective and to respect the views of others. Kegan's highest order of consciousness involves a process of transforming the very relationship with one's own position. Kegan explains that this episteme approaches systemic thought as necessarily partial, conditioned, and ultimately unworthy of one's entire identity.[34]

31. Caputo, *What Would Jesus Deconstruct?*, 62.
32. Barbour, *Versions of Deconversion*; Streib, *Deconversion*.
33. Harris, *Teaching and Religious Imagination*, 65, 72–73.
34. Kegan, *In Over Our Heads*, 319.

Deconversion and a Durable Good

Jackie's response to the language of "Secular Catholicism" is a poignant example of this contemporary meaning making. Her current views and practices demonstrate that her identification with Catholic tradition is now an object relation. She holds her learned sense of Catholic tradition at arm's length and is capable and confident to deconstruct and reconstruct it based on her views of what matters most and why. Her Catholicness is not the Catholicism that conventional authorities emphasize because she has learned the provisional nature of that expression. That said, even her sense of tradition does not constitute her entire identity. Jackie explained that she liked the language of "Secular Catholic" because it "gets her honest" about the hybrid nature of her religious practices and belonging. She shared further that most of her family—including a priest and religious studies professor—probably "lives there too."

This deconversion from conventional expectations represents a process of moving out from "taken-for-granted-ness" of external authority. Kegan suggests that this epistemic change in subject-object relations drives learning and growth toward more complex ways of knowing appropriate for the contemporary cultural circumstances.[35] Boys suggests that religious education, done in the reality of the contemporary pluralistic and liquid world, teaches embarrassment at absolutism and provides learners with tools for deconstructing knowledge to which they were once subject.[36] Caputo suggests that this shared faithful but critical activity of both deconstruction and reconstruction on behalf of experience and what a sense of tradition promises actually embodies a truer form of being religious.[37]

The religious educators and their disaffiliating former students demonstrate this process of encountering difference, deconstructing convention, and constructively determining what is essential and nonessential in terms of religious practice and identity. With or without ecclesial approval, this ongoing movement of deconversion is a significant part of who they have become religiously.

---

35. Kegan, *In Over Our Heads*, 34.
36. Boys, *Has God Only One Blessing?*, 27.
37. Caputo, *What Would Jesus Deconstruct?*, 55–56.

chapter 6

WHY DECONVERSION MATTERS

A Practical Discussion for Ministries with Young Adults

A new array of religious practices and identities is forming as more people move through and around modern expectations of single religious identity and affiliation. This fluidity constitutes a new normal. Even those who view this deinstitutionalization of religion as a crisis acknowledge that religious institutions are lagging behind the fluidity and diversity of everyday experience. Together, this perceived disconnection of the Catholic Church from everyday life, the very real crisis of moral authority, along with significant ethical differences regarding social questions has sent many young adults beyond church teaching and communities in search of meaning and authentic relationships.

Despite the powerful and potentially positive elements of Bauman's description of a "liquid modernity," his view is deeply pessimistic.[1] Bauman and others are concerned that today's more fluid options and norms exemplified at the edge of religious affiliation dissolve the structures that have kept communities together for thousands of years. In the case of religious disaffiliation, many faith leaders today similarly, and rightly, ask, "What will remain of our traditions if this movement continues?" "How could this not be a crisis?" These cautious perspectives begin from unquestionably and perhaps uncritical affiliated religious positions. As a result, their theological and methodological choices make it difficult to develop adequate frameworks to understand the dynamic forms of religiousness in the United States. They characterize the moral and spiritual life and learning that occurs beyond the edge of church affiliation as deviating from

---

1. Bauman, *Liquid Modernity*.

convention and therefore as deviant or "non" religious. Yet in fact research, like the portraits presented in this book, suggests that liquid modernity does not exclude continuity with the past or with tradition. At the very least, it is worth a second look, and more listening.

To give that effort a theological perspective, I offer a contrasting interpretation of "liquid modernity" for theologians and educators.

In Matthew 14:25–31, a mysterious figure approaches Peter and the apostles walking on the waters. When the apostles saw Jesus of Nazareth walking toward them, Peter's intuitive test to discern if it was in fact their teacher was to ask the figure to command him, Peter, to do the same—to step out from the security of the known (Matt 14:26–29). The Gospel episode implies that if the figure had told Peter to stay attached to the conventional security of the boat, Peter would have known it was not his teacher.

Though he recognized the significance of the invitation, Peter resisted the challenging call to leave behind that to which he had become accustomed. In the words of this book's preface, you might say that Peter could not yet let go of the security of the raft.

The story of Peter asking Jesus to command him to come to him out on waters provides both the generative metaphor and a theological perspective concerning finding our way in the contemporary context of "liquid modernity." What we often forget is that Peter did step out onto waters and even walked for a few steps.

STEPPING OUT TO MEET THEM

You might, like Peter, doubt the possibility of religiousness out there in liquid modernity. But, you have read this far. What sunk Cephas like a stone was that he resisted such an adjustment to his reality, and lacked a more complete affirming hope in what his teacher had come to promise. While ultimately he failed, Peter's initial faith reveals what he had come to trust. He expected Jesus to do the unexpected, and to invite his followers to do the same.

Peter and the disciples often struggled (like we do) to meet or understand the unexpected movements of Jesus in faith. The portraits offer a similar encounter, inviting and preparing the Catholic Church's educational ministries to respond better to the unexpected religious lives of deconverts today—by stepping out on the waters of liquid modernity for the same reason Peter did.

Divinity calls Peter to this precarious and productive place. Peter fails because he is afraid.

The contrast between the pessimistic view of liquid modernity and this more affirming image of Matthew 14 suggests that teachers and leaders might better respond to the religious lives of those living and learning in this edge that is a place by stepping out on the waters.

To be fair to Peter, his fear is reasonable. To be fair to critics concerned with liquid modernity, their fears are reasonable. As educators and theologians, like Peter we find ourselves out on a body of water for which we need a more up-to-date language that reflects the more liquid reality in which we live. I invite you to take similar steps as the educators portrayed have.

To take those steps, this chapter invites you to trust that G*d plays a role in the conversations stretching and re-interpreting the Christian tradition in particular times and places, and to join conversations like the ones portrayed. This Gospel scene of Matthew 14 also mirrors the experiences of the portrayed educators from whom we can learn.

Like Peter, although she had volunteered to participate in the research with her former student, Theresa doubted the possibility of religious life and learning out there on the waters. However, in and through the encounter with Jackie, she was willing to adjust her view to remain in relationship with her former student and her idea of the Divine, whom she could not deny might be at work in Jackie's life. When I asked Theresa whether she thought the religious education that occurred in her relationship with Jackie was successful, Theresa did not know how to say yes, but she could not say no either. Like the ease with which Eliot put Michael's religious life "in the win column," Theresa's honesty has much to teach Church leaders and teachers.

To Theresa's credit, when invited she did take a few steps out. She did not cry out, nor did she sink. She was open to the possibility that she was encountering the unexpected. In many ways I believe she was already out there, on waters—and so might be many other vital and effective educators and theologians who simply do not yet have a language to describe where they are and how they got there. The ability to name the processes involved in our own religious learning and teaching will better enable educators and theologians to take similar steps to meet those calling them out onto liquid modernity.

WHAT THE PORTRAITS REVEAL AND WHY IT MATTERS

In the North American Catholic context, the movement of religious disaffiliation is one of the most significant and ongoing events in the last one hundred years of religious history. Many characterize this exodus as a crisis. Is it? The conversations between teachers of religion and their former students witnessed in this book do reveal teaching-learning relationships exist in which the theological and pedagogical goals have less to do with an affiliated outcome as with handing on a faithful but critical sense of tradition, and practical religious knowledge. The portraits suggest a praxis-over-propositional approach that may be operative and optimal in many contemporary religious educational settings. Moreover, they demonstrate that one possible (and possibly positive) outcome of this form of teaching religion is deconversion, or ongoing religious development beyond the boundaries of conventional communities.

The many conversations drawn upon to create the portraits demonstrate that learning religion in liquid modernity involves inheriting a shared tradition, receiving insights from various relationships and extra-ecclesial experiences, testing what is good, and moving beyond what is not. Moreover, it is not only the disaffiliating young adults that embody this pattern of religious practice and identity. The portraits reveal that both teachers and learners are moving out from the taken-for-granted-ness of convention and onto unforeseen possibilities because they are called to do so by the everyday relationships in which they experience the Divine. They reveal that liquid modernity has expanded and made more viable a space at the edge of affiliation where a faithful but critical praxis can continue outside of the established boundaries of religious communities.

With these findings in mind, I introduced the language of deconversion to replace the pejorative narrative of loss and theology of affiliation limiting the understanding of ongoing religious life and learning outside the boundaries of conventional religious communities.

The portraits presented offer readers entry into the edge that is a place and the deconversion process that brings some people there. Although they are not exhaustive, the portraits make the complexity of that place and process more tangible, more personal, and more real. And, there are more conversations to be had. Those conversations begin in the same way these portraits did—by looking at ourselves and recognizing that our stories also push the boundaries of preconfigured religious categories.

In the first known Christian text of pastoral theology or religious education, St. Gregory the Great describes the effort as the "art of arts" because it is the care of souls.[2] Gregory suggests that the first step in good teaching ministry is to learn what is happening in the lives of learners—not what a teacher or the Church thinks is happening, or thinks ought to happen. Gregory suggests that this "art" includes accepting the possibility that learners may reject elements of our teaching if those elements do not correspond to the world in which they live.[3]

Owning this artistic part of our role in caring for souls involves looking honestly and critically at ourselves, and letting go of fabricated aspects of our work. We are the same complicated creature we are setting out to study. Accepting this less than objective but no less significant role in the art of arts is an important step in developing the capacity to let go of assumptions and co-create more life-giving theologies. Beaudoin calls this exercise "catching up to ourselves." Contemporary theology and religious education will benefit from us having the courage to question how we became who and how we are, and the assumptions involved in giving that perspective objective authority.[4] From this reflexivity, we can name not only who we are and how we became that way, but also what that becoming and location may reveal and contribute to our fields. In so doing, this personal work provides a practical point of departure for those interested in taking conscious and faithful steps in liquid modernity.

For the educators portrayed here, "catching up" to themselves has included exploring the theologically significant factors that formed them and identifying that some of those experiences have moved them beyond doctrinal or ecclesial boundaries. That "is really how it plays out," even for affiliated Catholics. "Catching up to ourselves" involves listening for the stories in our lives that move around static teachings or fixed interpretation of faith like water around a rock. Peter in the Gospel of Matthew offers a cautionary tale for this critical self-reflection.

Unlike Peter, the teachers and learners portrayed here were open to transformation. The religious educators and learners encountered in this research show each other how to be religious in the contemporary context. Instead of only teaching authorized doctrine, the vocation of educators and theologians today includes what Beaudoin theorizes as

2. See *The Book of Pastoral Rule*.
3. *The Book of Pastoral Rule*.
4. Beaudoin, *Witness to Dispossession*, 68.

"dispossession," or letting go of some of the stories we and the church have told ourselves about ourselves.[5] When we teachers and leaders can self-critically unearth those stories, we can enter into teaching-learning relationships with a resulting theological humility. That work readies us to step out on waters in faith.

Such willingness undergirds good religious education. Such critical self- and collective reflection work calls theologians and educators to identify with and learn from persons who have developed non-normative religious identities and practices *from* the same traditional teaching practices and movements that have formed us. This "catching up to ourselves" and "dispossession" brings us closer to what really matters to us and why. It also therefore brings us closer to the life G*d animates in us to share with others.

CATCHING UP TO MYSELF

As I explained in the preface, the questions explored in this book are drawn from my personal as well as my professional experiences. As a teacher, I have witnessed some of my strongest students leave the church. I find meaning and orientation in the story of Gautama Buddha teaching his disciples that they must learn to apply his teachings in an intelligent manner in varied situations, that his finger is only pointing at the moon, that the "raft" of his teaching is needed to reach the other shore but is not the shore itself.

My own desire as a teacher has been to share what I find so life-giving and interesting about religion, and about the Catholic tradition in particular. I love "pointing at the moon." I love "building the raft," and I have learned to love "letting it go." In and through this process, my students—perhaps especially the deconverts—have taught me how and where G*d is calling them, and therefore where I might look to renew my own faith. When a teacher or student or church mistakes their finger for the moon or the raft for what is promised across the waters, the life-giving encounter with G*d is lost.

---

5. Beaudoin, *Witness to Dispossession*.

Out On Waters—The Edge That Is a Place

WHAT DECONVERSION MEANS FOR THE CHURCH AND MINISTRY

In this more fluid cultural space in which we live, we now face an invitation and challenge to step out faithfully and encounter unexpected and innovating expressions of faith and tradition.

The portraits of Theresa, Eliot, James, and Maria show that Catholicness is being taught and learned in innovating and/or promising ways at the very intersection of preservation and revelation. The image of Peter sitting on the edge of that boat provides a provocative theological image for the church and ministry poised in a similar place. Peter knew that the movement toward the unexpected was an accurate test of what Christ's presence promised, but he lacked sufficient faith to take the steps. For Peter, upending the known order of things was too fraught and threatening to sustain. Understandably, he cried out, reached for the raft, and sunk like a rock. Jesus' response was compassionate but he was clearly disappointed.

We the Gospel readers are left with the question, "What did Peter miss by being of little faith out on those waters?" Christ has issued us the same invitation to step out, but with an added challenge: we know Peter's failure.

To depotentiate that fear and to allow affirming hope in the promise of our tradition to return, I suggest remembering that religious tradition has always developed as its members step out to respond to the world in which they live and where they experience the Divine. Deconversion, this activity of choosing what is essential and nonessential in religious practice and identity, often in contradiction to authoritative teaching, drives how we get somewhere religiously. Religious pedagogy and theology mindful of this tendency does not insist on or defend old positions, but on teaching our tradition in life-giving ways.

As the movements of deconversion increasingly influence religiousness in the United States, there will be nothing more valuable for educators and theologians to do than to learn the lesson Peter did. We need a means to overcome our fear and replace it with Peter's initial faith and hope. Remaining attached to the security of conventional religious expectations keeps education and theology stuck in similarly unmoving paradigms.

While there is a growing body of deconversion literature and more sociological research on the Nones, Beaudoin's suggestion of dispossession[6] and Gregory Baker's book proposing an apophatic ministry

---

6. Beaudoin, *Witness to Dispossession*.

on college campuses[7] are the only works I have encountered that suggest interventions that do not attempt to sustain affiliation. Baker also encourages a praxis-over-propositional effort fostering in ministers the ability to appreciate in themselves and their students a relationship with an unknown G*d. The pastoral and educational intervention he proposes serves the holistic growth of students without needing to reproduce conventional religious identity and practice.[8]

Teachers and leaders may need more help or time to engage the suggestion that disaffiliation is not a problem to solve. Approaches to research and ministry like Baker's, Beaudoin, and my own offer other practitioners a way to name what is happening as something other than a loss and a lens through which to understand disaffiliation as an alternative trajectory of ongoing religious life and learning. More than that, this more affirming and curious approach offers a way for interested fields to trust that these deconversions may be ongoing expressions of faith and tradition.

The Christian Story is not yet complete. G*d's activity in each new time and place calls for its own authentic response.[9] Authentic Christian faith is, then, open to conversation, literally. It is clear that more and more people are developing the freedom and confidence to move into this edge that is a place and move around the Church's influence like water around a rock. There are promising opportunities in the expressions of the Gospel and tradition found in the lives of deconverting Catholics, and there are ambiguities. I invite the reader to wonder with me, rather than to characterize the choice to disaffiliate as only a sign of deficiency.

CONTINUING THE CONVERSATION

This research portraiture has been concerned with offering a constructive theological and more affirming alternative for theologians and educators to allow into their research, writing, and practice in this time of liquid modernity. The resources and practices of our tradition that we hand over to our learners in our ministries are life-giving because they can craft new ways of moving in and through the world as it is (not as we think it ought to remain). There is no doubt that in stepping out to meet those living these alternative or innovative expressions of Catholicness we will be

---

7. See Baker, *Disaffiliating Ministry*.
8. Baker, *Disaffiliating Ministry*.
9. Groome, *Sharing Faith*, 48, 194.

changed, and by this I mean the church will be changed. That is my hope, because I see reason to trust we can do so faithfully. Many of us might already be stepping out onto the waters because it's only there that we have been able to find our way. What we find there should not be so surprising. If we live in liquid modernity, that is where the G*d of our tradition's understanding will be also. It is only from this precarious and promising place that we can find our way together.

It seems significant and maybe urgent to create dialogical spaces and encounters as in the foregoing portraits that can bring out the tacit conventions, such as the narrative of loss and theology of affiliation, that do not reflect the lives of both teachers and learners today. All the voices portrayed reflect hybrid experiences including joys and struggles of living and learning religiously. Taking these hybrid voices seriously as sources of theological knowledge requires a more modest role for conventional and normative voices that resist stepping out on the waters. I propose that we can learn from the educators portrayed and create similar spaces where educators and theologians can "catch up to themselves" and where the taken-for-grantedness of affiliation can be tested.

During Theresa's conversation with Jackie, to make sense of the life she was encountering she pointed to the lives of the saints that are so important to her. Theresa suggested that people like these "oddballs" provide consistent alternative, irreverent, and creative paths of religious life and learning beyond the known map of being Catholic. Eliot similarly drew upon a modern mystic to express his learning through participating in this study. He quoted Merton: "My Lord God, I have no idea where I am going. I do not see the road ahead of me. . . . The fact that I think I am following your will does not mean I am actually doing so. But I believe that the desire to please you does in fact please you. . . . I know that if I do this you will lead me by the right road, though I know nothing about it. Therefore I trust you always."[10] These educators who sat with former deconverting students asked themselves questions we scholars will also want to explore further.

---

10. See Merton, *Dialogues with Silence*.

BIBLIOGRAPHY

Anderson, Shawna L., et al. "Dearly Departed: How Often Do Congregations Close?" *Journal for the Scientific Study of Religion* 47 (2008) 321–28. doi:10.1111/j.1468-5906.2008.00410.x.

Baker, Gregory. *Disaffiliating Ministry: Spiritual Growth, Gender, and Campus Ministry*. Lanham, MD: Lexington, 2019.

Barbour, John D. *Versions of Deconversion: Autobiography and the Loss of Faith*. Charlottesville: University Press of Virginia, 1994.

Bauman, Chad. "Conversion Careers, Conversions-For, and Conversion in the Study of Religion." *Religion and Culture Web Forum* (2012) 1–5. http://digitalcommons.butler.edu/facsch_papers/597/.

Bauman, Zygmunt. *Liquid Modernity*. Cambridge, UK: Polity, 2015.

Beaudoin, Tom. *Consuming Faith: Integrating Who We Are with What We Buy*. New York: Sheed & Ward, 2007.

———. "Deconversion and Disaffiliation in Contemporary US Roman Catholicism." *Horizons* 40 (2013) 255–62. doi:10.1017/hor.2013.75.

———. "Response to Elizabeth Drescher's 'Cosmopolitan Christianities: Lived Faith in the Land Beyond Religion.'" Lecture presented at Fordham University, October 12, 2016.

———. "Secular Catholicism and Practical Theology." *International Journal of Practical Theology* 15 (2011) 22–37.

———. *Virtual Faith: The Irreverent Spiritual Quest of Generation X*. San Francisco: Jossey-Bass, 2000.

———. *Witness to Dispossession: The Vocation of a Postmodern Theologian*. Maryknoll: Orbis, 2008.

Beaudoin, Tom, and Patrick Hornbeck. "Deconversion and Catholic Multiplicity." Lecture presented at the American Academy of Religion Annual Meeting, San Diego, November 2014.

Bellah, Robert N., et al. *Individualism & Commitment in American Life: Readings on the Themes of Habits of the Heart*. New York: Harper & Row, 1988.

Bender, Courtney. *The New Metaphysicals: Spirituality and the American Religious Imagination*. Chicago: University of Chicago Press, 2010.

Bibliography

Boyarin, Daniel. *Border Lines: The Partition of Judaeo-Christianity*. Philadelphia: University of Pennsylvania Press, 2004.

Boys, Mary C. "Conversion as a Foundation of Religious Education." *Religious Education* 77 (1982) 211–24.

———. *Has God Only One Blessing? Judaism as a Source of Christian Self-Understanding*. New York: Paulist, 2000.

Boys, Mary C., and Sara S. Lee. *Christians & Jews in Dialogue: Learning in the Presence of the Other*. Woodstock, VT: SkyLight Paths, 2006.

Byron, William J., and Charles Zech. "On Their Way Out: What Exit Interviews Could Tell Us about Lapsed Catholics." *America*, January 2011.

Calder, Nigel. *How to Read a Nautical Chart: A Complete Guide to Using and Understanding Electronic and Paper Charts*. New York: McGraw-Hill Professional, 2012.

Caputo, John D. *What Would Jesus Deconstruct? The Good News of Postmodernity for the Church*. Grand Rapids: Baker Academic, 2007.

CARA. "Sacraments Today: Belief and Practice among U.S. Catholics." *Sacraments Today: Belief and Practice among U.S. Catholics*, 2008. http://cara.georgetown.edu/sacraments.html.

Cohn, D'Vera, and Andrea Caumont. "10 Demographic Trends That Are Shaping the U.S. and the World." *Pew Research Center*. March 31, 2016. http://www.pewresearch.org/fact-tank/2016/03/31/10-demographic-trends-that-are-shaping-the-u-s-and-the-world/.

Conde-Frazier, Elizabeth. "Participatory Action Research." *The Wiley-Blackwell Companion to Practical Theology*, edited by Bonnie J. Miller-McLemore, 234–43. Oxford: Wiley-Blackwell, 2014.

Conn, Walter E. *Conversion, Perspectives on Personal and Social Transformation*. New York: Alba House, 1978.

Cooper, Betsy, et al. "Exodus: Why Americans Are Leaving Religion—and Why They're Unlikely to Come Back." Public Religion Research Institute, 2016.

Day, Abby. *Believing in Belonging: Belief and Social Identity in the Modern World*. Oxford: Oxford University Press, 2013.

Derrida, Jacques, and John D. Caputo. *Deconstruction in a Nutshell: A Conversation with Jacques Derrida*. New York: Fordham University Press, 2008.

Downey, Allen B. "Religious Affiliation, Education and Internet Use." *Religious Affiliation, Education and Internet Use*. March 21, 2014. https://arxiv.org/abs/1403.5534.

Drescher, Elizabeth. *Choosing Our Religion: The Spiritual Lives of America's Nones*. New York: Oxford University Press, 2016.

Ebaugh, Helen Rose Fuchs. *Becoming an Ex: The Process of Role Exit*. Chicago: University of Chicago Press, 1998.

Elie, Paul. *The Life You Save May Be Your Own: An American Pilgrimage*. New York: Farrar, Straus and Giroux, 2004.

Fazekas, Andrew. "Voyager at the Edge: Cosmic Roadtrip Hits Milestone." *National Geographic Society* (blogs), December 6, 2012. http://voices.nationalgeographic.com/2012/12/06/voyager-at-the-edge-cosmic-roadtrip-hits-milestone/.

Fletcher, Jeannine Hill. "Religious Pluralism in an Era of Globalization: The Making of Modern Religious Identity." *Theological Studies* 69 (2008) 394–411.

Garland, David. "What Is a 'History of the Present'? On Foucault's Genealogies and Their Critical Preconditions." *Punishment & Society* 16 (2014) 365–84.

Bibliography

Gooren, H. *Religious Conversion and Disaffiliation: Tracing Patterns of Change in Faith Practices*. New York: Palgrave Macmillan, 2016.

Grant, Tobin. "Analysis: 7.5 Million Americans Lost Their Religion since 2012." *Religion News Service*, March 11, 2016.

Groome, Thomas H. *Christian Religious Education: Sharing Our Story and Vision*. Stockholm: TPB, 2019.

———. *Sharing Faith: A Comprehensive Approach to Religious Education and Pastoral Ministry; The Way of Shared Praxis*. San Francisco: HarperSanFrancisco, 1991.

Grossman, Cathy Lynn. "How Catholic Are US Catholics? It's All in How You Measure." *Religion News Service*, January 27, 2016.

Hansen, David T. "Cosmopolitanism as Education: A Philosophy for Educators in Our Time." *Religious Education* 112 (2017) 207–16.

Harris, Maria. *Teaching and Religious Imagination: An Essay in the Theology of Teaching*. San Francisco: HarperSanFrancisco, 1991.

Hedges, Paul. "Multiple Religious Belonging after Religion: Theorizing Strategic Religious Participation in a Shared Religious Landscape as a Chinese Model." *Open Theology* 3 (2017) 48–72.

Helmenstine, Anne Marie. "What Does a Catalyst Do in a Chemical Reaction?" *ThoughtCo*. Accessed March 26, 2017. https://www.thoughtco.com/definition-of-catalyst-604402.

Horell, Harold Daly. "Cultural Postmodernity and Christian Faith Formation." *Horizons & Hopes: The Future of Religious Education*, edited by Thomas H. Groome and Harold Daly Horell, 81–108. Mahwah, NJ: Paulist, 2003.

Imperatori-Lee, Natalia. *Cuéntame: Narrative in the Ecclesial Present*. Maryknoll: Orbis, 2018.

Irvin, Dale T. *Christian Histories, Christian Traditioning: Rendering Accounts*. Maryknoll: Orbis, 1998.

James, William. *The Varieties of Religious Experience: A Study in Human Nature*. New York: Modern Library, 1936.

Jamieson, Alan. *A Churchless Faith: Faith Journeys beyond the Churches*. London: SPCK, 2003.

Kegan, Robert. *In Over Our Heads: The Mental Demands of Modern Life*. Cambridge: Harvard University Press, 1994.

Landau, Elizabeth. "NASA Confirms Voyager 1 Probe Has Left the Solar System." *CNN*, October 2, 2013. http://www.cnn.com/2013/09/12/tech/innovation/voyager-solar-system/.

Lash, Nicholas. "Teaching of Commanding: When Bishops Instruct the Faithful." *America*, December 10, 2010.

Lawrence-Lightfoot, Sara, and Jessica Hoffmann Davis. *The Art and Science of Portraiture*. San Francisco: Jossey-Bass, 2002.

Lipka, Michael. "A Closer Look at America's Rapidly Growing Religious 'Nones.'" *Pew Research Center*. May 13, 2015. http://www.pewresearch.org/fact-tank/2015/05/13/a-closer-look-at-americas-rapidly-growing-religious-nones/.

———. "Millennials Increasingly Are Driving Growth of 'Nones.'" *Pew Research Center*. May 12, 2015. http://www.pewresearch.org/fact-tank/2015/05/12/millennials-increasingly-are-driving-growth-of-nones/.

BIBLIOGRAPHY

Lipka, Michael, and Claire Gecewicz. "More Americans Now Say They're Spiritual but Not Religious." *Pew Research Center.* September 6, 2017. http://www.pewresearch.org/fact-tank/2017/09/06/more-americans-now-say-theyre-spiritual-but-not-religious/.

Liu, Joseph. "The Global Religious Landscape." *Pew Research Center's Religion & Public Life Project.* December 17, 2012. http://www.pewforum.org/2012/12/18/global-religious-landscape-exec/.

———. "'Nones' on the Rise." *Pew Research Center's Religion & Public Life Project.* October 8, 2012. http://www.pewforum.org/2012/10/09/nones-on-the-rise/.

———. "Religion among the Millennials." *Pew Research Center's Religion Public Life Project.* February 17, 2010. http://www.pewforum.org/2010/02/17/religion-among-the-millennials/.

———. "Religious Switching and Intermarriage." *Pew Research Center's Religion & Public Life Project.* July 18, 2012. http://www.pewforum.org/2012/07/19/asian-americans-a-mosaic-of-faiths-religious-switching-and-intermarriage/.

Loder, James E. *The Transforming Moment: Understanding Convictional Experiences.* San Francisco: Harper & Row, 1981.

Masci, David, and Michael Lipka. "Americans May Be Getting Less Religious, but Feelings of Spirituality Are on the Rise." *Pew Research Center.* January 21, 2016. http://www.pewresearch.org/fact-tank/2016/01/21/americans-spirituality/.

Maynard, Jane Frances, et al. *Pastoral Bearings: Lived Religion and Pastoral Theology.* Lanham, MD: Lexington, 2011.

McGinn, Bernard. *The Essential Writings of Christian Mysticism.* New York: Modern Library, 2006.

Mead, Sidney Earl. *The Lively Experiment: The Shaping of Christianity in America.* New York: Harper & Row, 1963.

Merton, Thomas, and Jonathan Montaldo. *Dialogues with Silence: Prayers & Drawings.* San Francisco: HarperOne, 2006.

Miller, Susan Katz. *Being Both: Embracing Two Religions in One Interfaith Family.* Boston: Beacon, 2013.

Mitchell, Travis. "Americans Express Increasingly Warm Feelings toward Religious Groups." *Pew Research Center's Religion & Public Life Project.* February 15, 2017. http://www.pewforum.org/2017/02/15/americans-express-increasingly-warm-feelings-toward-religious-groups/.

Moran, Gabriel. *Religious Education Development: Images for the Future.* Minneapolis: Winston, 1983.

Nagle, James Michael. "How We Get Somewhere Religiously: Religious Education and Deconversion." *Religious Education* (2017) 1–9.

Navas, Eduardo. *Remix Theory: The Aesthetics of Sampling.* N.p.: Ambra Verlag, 2013.

Navas, Eduardo, et al. *The Routledge Companion to Remix Studies.* Abingdon, UK: Routledge, 2016.

Newport, Frank. "Questions and Answers about Americans' Religion." *Gallup.com.* December 24, 2007. http://www.gallup.com/poll/103459/Questions-Answers-About-Americans-Religion.aspx.

Paulson, Michael. "Even as U.S. Hispanics Lift Catholicism, Many Are Leaving the Church Behind." *New York Times,* May 7, 2014. https://www.nytimes.com/2014/05/08/upshot/even-as-hispanics-lift-catholicism-theyre-leaving-it.html.

Peace, Richard V. *Conversion in the New Testament: Paul and the Twelve.* Grand Rapids: Eerdmans, 2001.

Bibliography

Pelikan, Jaroslav. *The Vindication of Tradition*. New Haven, CT: Yale University Press, 1984.

Percy, Emma. *Mothering as a Metaphor for Ministry*. Farnham, UK: Ashgate, 2014.

Perl, Paul, and Mark Gray. "Catholic Schooling and Disaffiliation from Catholicism." *Journal for the Scientific Study of Religion* 46 (2007) 269–80.

Pew. "U.S. Religious Landscape Survey: Religious Affiliation." *Pew Forum on Religion & Public Life*. 2008. http://www.pewtrusts.org/en/research-and-analysis/reports/2008/02/25/us-religious-landscape-survey-religious-affiliation.

———. "U.S. Religious Landscape Survey: Religious Affiliation: Diverse and Dynamic." 2008. *Pew Forum on Religion & Public Life*. doi:http://www.pewforum.org/files/2013/05/report-religious-landscape-study-full.pdf.

Pope Paul VI. "Evangeli Nuntiandi." *Vatican Website*. December 8, 1975. http://w2.vatican.va/content/paul-vi/en/apost_exhortations/documents/hf_p-vi_exh_19751208_evangelii-nuntiandi.html.

Putnam, Robert D. *Bowling Alone: The Collapse and Revival of American Community*. New York: Simon & Schuster, 2007.

Ramey, Steven, and Monica Miller. "Meaningless Surveys: The Faulty Mathematics of the Nones." *Culture on the Edge: A Peer Reviewed Blog*, January 13, 2017. https://edge.ua.edu/steven-ramey/meaningless-surveys-the-faulty-mathematics-of-the-nones/.

Schmidt-Leukel, Perry. *Transformation by Integration: How Inter-Faith Encounter Changes Christianity*. London: SCM, 2009.

Schneiders, Laurel C. *Beyond Monotheism: A Theology of Multiplicity*. London: Routledge, 2008.

Schroeder, Carrie J. "The U.S. Conference of Catholic Bishops' Doctrinal Elements of a Curriculum Framework for the Development of Catechetical Materials for Young People of High School Age: Pedagogical and Theological Perspectives of Religious Studies Teachers in U.S. Catholic Secondary Schools." EdD diss., University of San Francisco, 2013.

Smith, Christian, and Melinda Lundquist Denton. *Soul Searching: The Religious and Spiritual Lives of American Teenagers*. Oxford: Oxford University Press, 2011.

Smith, James K. A. *How (Not) to Be Secular: Reading Charles Taylor*. Grand Rapids: Eerdmans, 2015.

Spadaro, Antonio, and Marcelo Figueroa. "Evangelical Fundamentalism and Catholic Integralism: A Surprising Ecumenism." *La Civiltà Cattolica*, July 26, 2017. http://www.laciviltacattolica.it/articolo/evangelical-fundamentalism-and-catholic-integralism-in-the-usa-a-surprising-ecumenism/.

Stone, Edward. "NASA's Voyager 1 Reaches the 'Magnetic Highway.'" NPR, December 4, 2012. http://www.npr.org/2012/12/04/166519632/nasas-voyager-1-reaches-the-magnetic-highway.

Streib, Heinz. *Deconversion: Qualitative and Quantitative Results from Cross-Cultural Research in Germany and the United States of America*. Göttingen: Vandenhoeck & Ruprecht, 2009.

———. "Faith Development Theory Revisited: The Religious Styles Perspective." *International Journal for the Psychology of Religion* 11 (2017) 143–58.

Syverson, Andrea. "30 Million American Christians Are Keeping Faith, but Avoiding Church." *Sojourners*, July 6, 2017. https://sojo.net/articles/30-million-american-christians-are-keeping-faith-avoiding-church.

Bibliography

Tauber, Sarah M. *Open Minds, Devoted Hearts: Portraits of Adult Religious Educators.* Eugene, OR: Pickwick, 2015.

Taylor, Charles. *A Secular Age.* Cambridge: Belknap Press of Harvard University Press, 2007.

Thiemann, Ronald F. *Religion in Public Life: A Dilemma for Democracy.* Washington, DC: Georgetown University Press, 1996.

Tweed, Thomas A. *Crossing and Dwelling: A Theory of Religion.* Cambridge: Harvard University Press, 2008.

United States Conference of Catholic Bishops. "Doctrinal Elements of a Curriculum Framework for the Development of Catechetical Materials for Young People of High School Age." *United States Conference of Catholic Bishops*, 2008. http://www.usccb.org/beliefs-and-teachings/how-we-teach/catechesis/upload/high-school-curriculum-framework.pdf.

Whitehead, James D., and Evelyn Eaton Whitehead. *Method in Ministry: Theological Reflection and Christian Ministry.* Franklin, WI: Sheed & Ward, 1999.

Williams, Terry Tempest. *Refuge: An Unnatural History of Family and Place.* Vintage, 1991.

Winter, Miriam Therese, et al. *Defecting in Place: Women Claiming Responsibility for Their Own Spiritual Lives.* New York: Crossroad, 1995.

Wormald, Benjamin. "Religious Landscape Study." *Pew Research Center's Religion Public Life Project.* May 11, 2015. http://www.pewforum.org/religious-landscape-study/religious-tradition/unaffiliated-religious-nones/.

Wuerl, Donald W. *New Evangelization: Passing on the Catholic Faith Today.* Huntington, IN: Our Sunday Visitor, 2013.

www.ingramcontent.com/pod-product-compliance
Lightning Source LLC
Chambersburg PA
CBHW070915160426
43193CB00011B/1463